FOREWORD

The collection of "Everything Will Be Okay" travel phrasebooks published by T&P Books is designed for people traveling abroad for tourism and business. The phrasebooks contain what matters most - the essentials for basic communication. This is an indispensable set of phrases to "survive" while abroad.

This phrasebook will help you in most cases where you need to ask something, get directions, find out how much something costs, etc. It can also resolve difficult communication situations where gestures just won't help.

This book contains a lot of phrases that have been grouped according to the most relevant topics. A separate section of the book also provides a small dictionary with more than 1,500 important and useful words.

Take "Everything Will Be Okay" phrasebook with you on the road and you'll have an irreplaceable traveling companion who will help you find your way out of any situation and teach you to not fear speaking with foreigners.

TABLE OF CONTENTS

T&P Books Publishing

T&P Books Publishing

PHRASEBOOK
- AFRIKAANS -

THE MOST IMPORTANT PHRASES

This phrasebook contains
the most important
phrases and questions
for basic communication
Everything you need
to survive overseas

By Andrey Taranov

T&P BOOKS

Phrasebook + 1500-word dictionary

English-Afrikaans phrasebook & concise dictionary

By Andrey Taranov

The collection of "Everything Will Be Okay" travel phrasebooks published by T&P Books is designed for people traveling abroad for tourism and business. The phrasebooks contain what matters most - the essentials for basic communication. This is an indispensable set of phrases to "survive" while abroad.

Another section of the book also provides a small dictionary with more than 1,500 useful words arranged alphabetically. The dictionary includes a lot of gastronomic terms and will be helpful when ordering food at a restaurant or buying groceries at the store.

T&P Books Publishing
www.tpbooks.com

ISBN: 978-1-78716-572-4

This book is also available in E-book formats.
Please visit www.tpbooks.com or the major online bookstores.

PRONUNCIATION

T&P phonetic alphabet	Afrikaans example	English example
[a]	land	shorter than in ask
[ā]	straat	calf, palm
[æ]	hout	chess, man
[o], [ɔ]	Australië	drop, baught
[e]	metaal	elm, medal
[ɛ]	aanlê	man, bad
[ə]	filter	driver, teacher
[ɪ]	uur	big, America
[i]	billik	shorter than in feet
[ī]	naïef	tree, big
[o]	koppie	pod, John
[ø]	akteur	eternal, church
[œ]	fluit	German Hölle
[u]	hulle	book
[ʊ]	hout	good, booklet
[b]	bakker	baby, book
[d]	donder	day, doctor
[f]	navraag	face, food
[g]	burger	game, gold
[h]	driehoek	home, have
[j]	byvoeg	yes, New York
[k]	kamera	clock, kiss
[l]	loon	lace, people
[m]	môre	magic, milk
[n]	neef	sang, thing
[p]	pyp	pencil, private
[r]	rigting	rice, radio
[s]	oplos	city, boss
[t]	lood, tenk	tourist, trip
[v]	bewaar	very, river
[w]	oorwinnaar	vase, winter
[z]	zoem	zebra, please
[dʒ]	enjin	joke, general
[ʃ]	artisjok	machine, shark
[ŋ]	kans	English, ring

T&P phonetic alphabet	Afrikaans example	English example
[tʃ]	tjek	church, French
[ʒ]	beige	forge, pleasure
[x]	agent	as in Scots 'loch'

LIST OF ABBREVIATIONS

English abbreviations

ab.	-	about
adj	-	adjective
adv	-	adverb
anim.	-	animate
as adj	-	attributive noun used as adjective
e.g.	-	for example
etc.	-	et cetera
fam.	-	familiar
fem.	-	feminine
form.	-	formal
inanim.	-	inanimate
masc.	-	masculine
math	-	mathematics
mil.	-	military
n	-	noun
pl	-	plural
pron.	-	pronoun
sb	-	somebody
sing.	-	singular
sth	-	something
v aux	-	auxiliary verb
vi	-	intransitive verb
vi, vt	-	intransitive, transitive verb
vt	-	transitive verb

T&P BOOKS

AFRIKAANS
PHRASEBOOK

This section contains
important phrases that may
come in handy in various
real-life situations.
The phrasebook will help
you ask for directions, clarify
a price, buy tickets, and
order food at a restaurant

T&P Books Publishing

PHRASEBOOK CONTENTS

T&P Books Publishing

The bare minimum

Excuse me, ... | **Verskoon my, ...**
[ferskoən maj, ...]

Hello. | **Hallo.**
[hallo.]

Thank you. | **Baie dankie.**
[baje danki.]

Good bye. | **Totsiens.**
[totsiŋs.]

Yes. | **Ja.**
[ja.]

No. | **Nee.**
[neə.]

I don't know. | **Ek weet nie.**
[ɛk veet ni.]

Where? | Where to? | When? | **Waar? | Waarheen? | Wanneer?**
[vãr? | vãrheən? | vanneər?]

I need ... | **Ek het ... nodig**
[ɛk het ... nodəχ]

I want ... | **Ek wil ...**
[ɛk vil ...]

Do you have ...? | **Het u ...?**
[het u ...?]

Is there a ... here? | **Is hier 'n ...?**
[is hir ə ...?]

May I ...? | **Mag ek ...?**
[maχ ek ...?]

..., please (polite request) | **... asseblief**
[... asseblif]

I'm looking for ... | **Ek soek ...**
[ɛk suk ...]

restroom | **toilet**
[tojlet]

ATM | **OTM**
[o·te·em]

pharmacy (drugstore) | **apteek**
[apteək]

hospital | **hospitaal**
[hospitãl]

police station | **polisiekantoor**
[polisi·kantoər]

subway | **moltrein**
[moltræjn]

taxi	**taxi** [taksi]
train station	**stasie** [stasi]

My name is ...	**My naam is ...** [maj nãm is ...]
What's your name?	**Wat is u naam?** [vat is u nãm?]
Could you please help me?	**Kan u my help, asseblief?** [kan u maj hɛlp, asseblif?]
I've got a problem.	**Ek het 'n probleem.** [ɛk het ə probleəm.]
I don't feel well.	**Ek voel nie lekker nie.** [ɛk ful ni lɛkkər ni.]
Call an ambulance!	**Bel 'n ambulans!** [bel ə ambulaŋs!]
May I make a call?	**Kan ek 'n oproep maak?** [kan ɛk ə oprup mãk?]

I'm sorry.	**Jammer.** [jammər.]
You're welcome.	**Plesier.** [plesir.]

I, me	**Ek, my** [ek, maj]
you (inform.)	**jy** [jaj]
he	**hy** [haj]
she	**sy** [saj]
they (masc.)	**hulle** [hullə]
they (fem.)	**hulle** [hullə]
we	**ons** [ɔŋs]
you (pl)	**julle** [jullə]
you (sg, form.)	**u** [u]

ENTRANCE	**INGANG** [inχaŋ]
EXIT	**UITGANG** [œitχaŋ]
OUT OF ORDER	**BUITE WERKING** [bœitə verkiŋ]
CLOSED	**GESLUIT** [χeslœit]

OPEN	**OOP**
	[oəp]
FOR WOMEN	**DAMES**
	[dames]
FOR MEN	**MANS**
	[maŋs]

Questions

Where?	**Waar?** [vãr?]
Where to?	**Waarheen?** [vãrheən?]
Where from?	**Van waar?** [fan vãr?]
Why?	**Waar?** [vãr?]
For what reason?	**Waarom?** [vãrom?]
When?	**Wanneer?** [vanneər?]
How long?	**Hoe lank?** [hu lank?]
At what time?	**Hoe laat?** [hu lãt?]
How much?	**Hoeveel?** [hufeəl?]
Do you have ...?	**Het u ...?** [het u ...?]
Where is ...?	**Waar is ...?** [vãr is ...?]
What time is it?	**Hoe laat is dit?** [hu lãt is dit?]
May I make a call?	**Kan ek 'n oproep maak?** [kan ɛk ə oprup mãk?]
Who's there?	**Wie is daar?** [vi is dãr?]
Can I smoke here?	**Mag ek hier rook?** [maχ ek hir roək?]
May I ...?	**Mag ek ...?** [maχ ek ...?]

Needs

I'd like ...	**Ek sou graag ...** [ɛk sæʊ χrāχ ...]
I don't want ...	**Ek wil nie ...** [ɛk vil ni ...]
I'm thirsty.	**Ek is dors.** [ɛk is dors.]
I want to sleep.	**Ek wil slaap.** [ɛk vil slāp.]
I want ...	**Ek wil ...** [ɛk vil ...]
to wash up	**was** [vas]
to brush my teeth	**my tande borsel** [maj tandə borsəl]
to rest a while	**bietjie rus** [biki rus]
to change my clothes	**ander klere aantrek** [andər klerə āntrek]
to go back to the hotel	**teruggaan hotel toe** [teruχχān hotəl tu]
to buy ...	**... koop** [... koəp]
to go to ...	**gaan na ...** [χān na ...]
to visit ...	**besoek ...** [besuk ...]
to meet with ...	**ontmoet ...** [ontmut ...]
to make a call	**bel** [bəl]
I'm tired.	**Ek is moeg.** [ɛk is muχ.]
We are tired.	**Ons is moeg.** [ɔŋs is muχ.]
I'm cold.	**Ek kry koud.** [ɛk kraj kæʊt.]
I'm hot.	**Ek kry warm.** [ɛk kraj varm.]
I'm OK.	**Ek is OK.** [ɛk is okej.]

I need to make a call.

Ek moet 'n oproep maak.
[ɛk mut ə oprup māk.]

I need to go to the restroom.

Ek moet toilet toe gaan.
[ɛk mut toilet tu χān.]

I have to go.

Ek moet loop.
[ɛk mut loəp.]

I have to go now.

Ek moet nou loop.
[ɛk mut næʊ loəp.]

Asking for directions

Excuse me, ...	**Verskoon tog, ...** [ferskoən toχ, ...]
Where is ...?	**Waar is ...?** [vãr is ...?]
Which way is ...?	**In watter rigting is ...?** [in vattər riχtiŋ is ...?]
Could you help me, please?	**Kan u my help, asseblief?** [kan u maj hɛlp, asseblif?]
I'm looking for ...	**Ek soek ...** [ɛk suk ...]
I'm looking for the exit.	**Waar is die uitgang?** [vãr is di œitχaŋ?]
I'm going to ...	**Ek gaan na ...** [ɛk χãn na ...]
Am I going the right way to ...?	**Is dit die regte pad na ...?** [is dit di reχtə pat na ...?]
Is it far?	**Is dit ver?** [is dit fer?]
Can I get there on foot?	**Kan ek te voet soontoe gaan?** [kan ɛk tə fut soentu χãn?]
Can you show me on the map?	**Kan u dit op die kaart aanwys?** [kan u dit op di kãrt ãnwajs?]
Show me where we are right now.	**Kan u my aanwys waar ons nou is?** [kan u maj ãnwajs vãr ɔŋs næʊ is?]
Here	**Hier** [hir]
There	**Daar** [dãr]
This way	**Hiernatoe** [hirnatu]
Turn right.	**Draai regs.** [drãj reχs.]
Turn left.	**Draai links.** [drãj links.]
first (second, third) turn	**eerste (tweede, derde) draai** [eərstə (tweədə, derde) drãi]

to the right   **na regs**
[na reχs]

to the left   **na links**
[na links]

Go straight ahead.   **Gaan reguit vorentoe.**
[χān reχœit forentu.]

Signs

WELCOME!	**WELKOM!** [vɛlkom!]
ENTRANCE	**INGANG** [inχaŋ]
EXIT	**UITGANG** [œitχaŋ]
PUSH	**STOOT** [stoət]
PULL	**TREK** [trek]
OPEN	**OOP** [oəp]
CLOSED	**GESLUIT** [χeslœit]
FOR WOMEN	**DAMES** [dames]
FOR MEN	**MANS (M)** [maŋs]
GENTLEMEN, GENTS (m)	**MANS (M)** [maŋs]
WOMEN (f)	**DAMES (V)** [dames]
DISCOUNTS	**AFSLAG** [afslaχ]
SALE	**UITVERKOPING** [œitferkopiŋ]
FREE	**GRATIS** [χratis]
NEW!	**NUUT!** [nɪt!]
ATTENTION!	**PAS OP!** [pas op!]
NO VACANCIES	**KAMERS BESET** [kamers beset]
RESERVED	**BESPREEK** [bespreək]
ADMINISTRATION	**ADMINISTRASIE** [administrasi]
STAFF ONLY	**SLEGS PERSONEEL** [sleχs personeəl]

BEWARE OF THE DOG!

PAS OP VIR DIE HOND
[pas op fir di hont]

NO SMOKING!

ROOK VERBODE!
[roək ferbodə!]

DO NOT TOUCH!

NIE AANRAAK NIE!
[ni ānrāk ni!]

DANGEROUS

GEVAARLIK
[χefārlik]

DANGER

GEVAAR
[χefār]

HIGH VOLTAGE

HOOGSPANNING
[hoəχ·spanniŋ]

NO SWIMMING!

SWEM VERBODE!
[swem ferbodə!]

OUT OF ORDER

BUITE GEBRUIK
[bœitə χebrœik]

FLAMMABLE

BRANDBAAR
[brantbār]

FORBIDDEN

VERBODE
[ferbodə]

NO TRESPASSING!

TOEGANG VERBODE!
[tuχaŋ ferbodə!]

WET PAINT

NAT VERF
[nat ferf]

CLOSED FOR RENOVATIONS

GESLUIT VIR HERSTELWERK
[χeslœit fir herstəl·werk]

WORKS AHEAD

PADWERKE
[padwerkə]

DETOUR

OMPAD
[ompat]

Transportation. General phrases

plane	**vliegtuig** [fliχtœix]
train	**trein** [træjn]
bus	**bus** [bus]
ferry	**veerboot** [feər·boət]
taxi	**taxi** [taksi]
car	**motor** [motor]

schedule	**diensrooster** [diŋs·roəstər]
Where can I see the schedule?	**Waar is die diensrooster?** [vãr is di diŋs·roəster?]
workdays (weekdays)	**werksdae** [verksdaə]
weekends	**naweke** [navekə]
holidays	**vakansies** [fakaŋsis]

DEPARTURE	**VERTREK** [fertrek]
ARRIVAL	**AANKOMS** [ãnkoms]
DELAYED	**VERTRAAG** [fertrãχ]
CANCELLED	**GEKANSELLEER** [χekaŋsɛlleər]

next (train, etc.)	**volgende** [folχendə]
first	**eerste** [eərstə]
last	**laaste** [lãstə]

When is the next …?	**Wanneer vertrek die volgende …?** [vanneər fertrek di folχendə …?]
When is the first …?	**Wanneer vertrek die eerste …?** [vanneər fertrek di eərstə …?]

When is the last ...?

Wanneer vertrek die laaste ...?
[vanneǝr fertrek di lāstǝ ...?]

transfer (change of trains, etc.)

aansluitlng
[āŋslœitiŋ]

to make a transfer

oorstap
[oǝrstap]

Do I need to make a transfer?

Moet ek oorstap?
[mut ek oǝrstap?]

Buying tickets

Where can I buy tickets?	**Waar kan ek kaartjies koop?** [vãr kan ɛk kãrkis koəp?]
ticket	**kaartjie** [kãrki]
to buy a ticket	**'n kaartjie koop** [ə kãrki koəp]
ticket price	**kaartjie se prys** [kãrki sə prajs]
Where to?	**Waarheen?** [vãrheən?]
To what station?	**Na watter stasie?** [na vattər stasi?]
I need ...	**Ek het ... nodig** [ɛk het ... nodəχ]
one ticket	**'n kaartjie** [ə kãrki]
two tickets	**twee kaartjies** [tweə kãrkis]
three tickets	**drie kaartjies** [dri kãrkis]
one-way	**enkel** [ɛnkəl]
round-trip	**retoer** [retur]
first class	**eerste klas** [eərstə klas]
second class	**tweede klas** [tweədə klas]
today	**vandag** [fandaχ]
tomorrow	**môre** [mɔrə]
the day after tomorrow	**oormôre** [oərmɔrə]
in the morning	**soggens** [soχɛŋs]
in the afternoon	**smiddags** [smiddaχs]
in the evening	**saans** [sãŋs]

aisle seat	**sitplek langs die paadjie** [sitplek laŋs di pādʒi]
window seat	**venstersitplek** [fɛŋstər·sitplek]
How much?	**Hoeveel?** [hufeəl?]
Can I pay by credit card?	**Kan ek met 'n kredietkaart betaal?** [kan ɛk met ə kreditkārt betāl?]

Bus

bus	**bus** [bus]
intercity bus	**interstedelike bus** [interstedelikə bus]
bus stop	**bushalte** [bus·haltə]
Where's the nearest bus stop?	**Waar is die naaste bushalte?** [vǎr is di nǎstə bus·haltə?]
number (bus ~, etc.)	**nommer** [nommər]
Which bus do I take to get to …?	**Watter bus moet ek neem om na … te gaan?** [vattər bus mut ɛk neəm om na … tə χǎn?]
Does this bus go to …?	**Gaan hierdie bus na …?** [χǎn hirdi bus na …?]
How frequent are the buses?	**Hoe gereëld ry die busse?** [hu χereɛlt raj di bussə?]
every 15 minutes	**elke 15 minute** [ɛlkə fajftin minutə]
every half hour	**elke half uur** [ɛlkə half ɪr]
every hour	**elke uur** [ɛlkə ɪr]
several times a day	**verskillende kere per dag** [ferskillendə kerə pər daχ]
… times a day	**… kere per dag** [… kerə pər daχ]
schedule	**diensrooster** [diŋs·roəstər]
Where can I see the schedule?	**Waar is die diensrooster?** [vǎr is di diŋs·roəstər?]
When is the next bus?	**Wanneer vertrek die volgende bus?** [vanneər fertrek di folχendə bus?]
When is the first bus?	**Wanneer vertrek die eerste bus?** [vanneər fertrek di eərstə bus?]
When is the last bus?	**Wanneer vertrek die laaste bus?** [vanneər fertrek di lǎstə bus?]

stop

halte
[haltə]

next stop

volgende halte
[folχendə haltə]

last stop (terminus)

eindpunt
[æjnd·punt]

Stop here, please.

Stop hier, asseblief.
[stop hir, asseblif.]

Excuse me, this is my stop.

Verskoon my, dis my halte.
[ferskoən maj, dis maj halte.]

Train

train	**trein** [træjn]
suburban train	**voorstedelike trein** [foərstedelikə træjn]
long-distance train	**langafstand trein** [lanχ·afstant træjn]
train station	**stasie** [stasi]
Excuse me, where is the exit to the platform?	**Verskoon my, waar is die uitgang na die perron?** [ferskoən maj, vār is di œitχaŋ na di perron?]

Does this train go to ...?	**Gaan hierdie trein na ...?** [χān hirdi træjn na ...?]
next train	**volgende trein** [folχendə træjn]
When is the next train?	**Wanneer vertrek die volgende trein?** [vanneər fertrek di folχendə træjn?]
Where can I see the schedule?	**Waar is die diensrooster?** [vār is di diŋs·roəster?]
From which platform?	**Van watter perron?** [fan vattər perron?]
When does the train arrive in ...?	**Wanneer kom die trein aan in ...?** [vanneər kom di træjn ān in ...?]

Please help me.	**Help my, asseblief.** [hɛlp maj, asseblif.]
I'm looking for my seat.	**Ek soek my sitplek.** [ɛk suk maj sitplek.]
We're looking for our seats.	**Ons soek ons sitplek.** [oŋs suk oŋs sitplek.]
My seat is taken.	**My sitplek is beset.** [maj sitplek is beset.]
Our seats are taken.	**Ons sitplekke is beset.** [oŋs sitplekkə is beset.]

I'm sorry but this is my seat.	**Jammer, dis my sitplek.** [jammər, dis maj sitplek.]
Is this seat taken?	**Is hierdie sitplek beset?** [is hirdi sitplek beset?]
May I sit here?	**Kan ek hier sit?** [kan ek hir sit?]

On the train. Dialogue (No ticket)

Ticket, please.	**Kaartjie, asseblief.** [kãrki, asseblif.]
I don't have a ticket.	**Ek het nie 'n kaartjie nie.** [ɛk het ni ə kãrki ni.]
I lost my ticket.	**Ek het my kaartjie verloor.** [ɛk het maj kãrki ferloər.]
I forgot my ticket at home.	**Ek het my kaartjie by die huis vergeet.** [ɛk het maj kãrki baj di hœis ferχeet.]
You can buy a ticket from me.	**U kan 'n kaartjie van my koop.** [u kan ə kãrki fan maj koəp.]
You will also have to pay a fine.	**U moet 'n boete betaal.** [u mut ə butə betãl.]
Okay.	**Oukei.** [æʊkæj.]
Where are you going?	**Waarheen gaan u?** [vãrheən χãn u?]
I'm going to ...	**Ek gaan na ...** [ɛk χãn na ...]
How much? I don't understand.	**Hoeveel kos dit? Ek verstaan dit nie.** [hufeəl kos dit? ek ferstãn dit ni.]
Write it down, please.	**Skryf dit neer, asseblief.** [skrajf dit neər, asseblif.]
Okay. Can I pay with a credit card?	**OK. Kan ek met 'n kredietkaart betaal?** [okej. kan ɛk met ə kreditkãrt betãl?]
Yes, you can.	**Ja, dit kan.** [ja, dit kan.]
Here's your receipt.	**Hier is u ontvangsbewys.** [hir is u ontfaŋs·bevajs.]
Sorry about the fine.	**Jammer vir die boete.** [jammər fir di bute.]
That's okay. It was my fault.	**Dis oukei. Dit was my skuld.** [dis æʊkæj. dit vas maj skult.]
Enjoy your trip.	**Geniet u reis.** [χenit u ræjs.]

Taxi

taxi	**taxi** [taksi]
taxi driver	**taxibestuurder** [taksi·bestɪrdər]
to catch a taxi	**'n taxi neem** [ə taksi neəm]
taxi stand	**taxistaanplek** [taksi·stānplek]
Where can I get a taxi?	**Waar kan ek 'n taxi neem?** [vãr kan ɛk ə taksi neəm?]
to call a taxi	**'n taxi bel** [ə taksi bəl]
I need a taxi.	**Ek het 'n taxi nodig.** [ɛk het ə taksi nodəχ.]

Right now.	**Nou onmiddellik.** [næʊ onmiddɛllik.]
What is your address (location)?	**Wat is u adres?** [vat is u adres?]
My address is …	**My adres is …** [maj adres is …]
Your destination?	**U bestemming?** [u bestɛmmiŋ?]
Excuse me, …	**Verskoon tog, …** [ferskoən toχ, …]
Are you available?	**Is u vry?** [is u fraj?]
How much is it to get to …?	**Hoeveel kos dit na …?** [hufeəl kos dit na …?]
Do you know where it is?	**Weet u waar dit is?** [veət u vãr dit is?]

Airport, please.	**Lughawe, asseblief** [luχhavə, asseblif]
Stop here, please.	**Stop hier, asseblief.** [stop hir, asseblif.]
It's not here.	**Dis nie hier nie.** [dis ni hir ni.]
This is the wrong address.	**Dis die verkeerde adres.** [dis di ferkeərdə adres.]
Turn left.	**Draai links.** [drãj links.]
Turn right.	**Draai regs.** [drãj reχs.]

How much do I owe you?

Wat skuld ek u?
[vat skult ek u?]

I'd like a receipt, please.

Kan ek 'n ontvangsbewys kry, asseblief?
[kan ek ə ontfaŋs·bevajs kraj, asseblif?]

Keep the change.

Hou die kleingeld.
[hæʊ di klæjŋ·χɛlt.]

Would you please wait for me?

Sal u vir my wag, asseblief?
[sal u fir maj vaχ, asseblif?]

five minutes

vyf minute
[fajf minutə]

ten minutes

tien minute
[tin minutə]

fifteen minutes

vyftien minute
[fajftin minutə]

twenty minutes

twintig minute
[twintəχ minutə]

half an hour

'n halfuur
[ə halfɪr]

Hotel

Hello.	**Hallo.**
	[hallo.]
My name is ...	**My naam is ...**
	[maj nãm is ...]
I have a reservation.	**Ek het bespreek.**
	[ɛk het bespreǝk.]

I need ...	**Ek het ... nodig**
	[ɛk het ... nodǝχ]
a single room	**'n enkelkamer**
	[ǝ ɛnkǝl·kamǝr]
a double room	**'n dubbelkamer**
	[ǝ dubbǝl·kamǝr]
How much is that?	**Hoeveel kos dit?**
	[hufeǝl kos dit?]
That's a bit expensive.	**Dis nogal duur.**
	[dis noχal dɪr.]

Do you have anything else?	**Is daar nie ander moontlikhede nie?**
	[is dãr ni andǝr moentlikhedǝ ni?]
I'll take it.	**Ek vat dit.**
	[ɛk fat dit.]
I'll pay in cash.	**Ek betaal kontant.**
	[ɛk betãl kontant.]

I've got a problem.	**Ek het 'n probleem.**
	[ɛk het ǝ probleǝm.]
My ... is broken.	**My ... is stukkend.**
	[maj ... is stukkent.]
My ... is out of order.	**My ... is buite werking.**
	[maj ... is bœitǝ verkiŋ.]
TV	**TV**
	[te·fe]
air conditioner	**lugreëling**
	[luχreɛliŋ]
tap	**kraan**
	[krãn]

shower	**stortbad**
	[stortbat]
sink	**wasbak**
	[vasbak]
safe	**brandkas**
	[brant·kas]

door lock	**deur se slot** [døər sə slot]
electrical outlet	**stopkontak** [stop·kontak]
hairdryer	**haardroër** [hār·droɛr]

I don't have …	**Ek het nie …** [ɛk het ni …]
water	**water** [vatər]
light	**lig** [liχ]
electricity	**krag** [kraχ]

Can you give me …?	**Kan u vir my … gee?** [kan u fir maj … χeə?]
a towel	**'n handdoek** [ə handduk]
a blanket	**'n kombers** [ə kombərs]
slippers	**pantoffels** [pantoffəls]
a robe	**'n kamerjas** [ə kamerjas]
shampoo	**sjampoe** [ʃampu]
soap	**seep** [seəp]

I'd like to change rooms.	**Ek wil van kamer verander.** [ɛk vil van kamər verandər.]
I can't find my key.	**Ek kan my sleutel nie vind nie.** [ɛk kan maj sløətəl ni fint ni.]
Could you open my room, please?	**Kan u my kamer oopsluit, asseblief?** [kan u maj kamər oəpslœit, asseblif?]
Who's there?	**Wie is daar?** [vi is dār?]
Come in!	**Kom binne!** [kom binnə!]
Just a minute!	**'n Oomblik!** [ə oəmblik!]
Not right now, please.	**Nie nou nie, asseblief.** [ni næʊ ni, asseblif.]

Come to my room, please.	**Kom na my kamer, asseblief.** [kom na maj kamər, asseblif.]
I'd like to order food service.	**Kan ek kamerbediening kry.** [kan ɛk kamər·bediniŋ kraj.]
My room number is …	**My kamer se nommer is …** [maj kamər sə nommer is …]

I'm leaving … **Ek vertrek …**
[ɛk fertrək …]

We're leaving … **Ons vertrek …**
[ɔŋs fertrek …]

right now **nou dadellik**
[næʊ dadɛllik]

this afternoon **vanmiddag**
[fanmiddaχ]

tonight **vanaand**
[fanãnt]

tomorrow **môre**
[mɔrə]

tomorrow morning **môreoggend**
[mɔrə·oχent]

tomorrow evening **môremiddag**
[mɔrə·middaχ]

the day after tomorrow **oormôre**
[oərmɔrə]

I'd like to pay. **Ek wil betaal.**
[ɛk vil betāl.]

Everything was wonderful. **Alles was uitstekend.**
[alles vas œitstekent.]

Where can I get a taxi? **Waar kan ek 'n taxi kry?**
[vãr kan ɛk ə taksi kraj?]

Would you call a taxi for me, please? **Sal u 'n taxi vir my bestel, asseblief.**
[sal u ə taksi fir maj bestel, asseblif.]

Restaurant

Can I look at the menu, please? **Kan ek die spyskaart sien, asseblief?**
[kan ɛk di spajskärt sin, asseblif?]

Table for one. **'n Tafel vir een persoon.**
[ə tafəl fir eən persoən.]

There are two (three, four) of us. **Daar is twee (drie, vier) van ons.**
[dār is tweə (dri, fir) fan ɔŋs.]

Smoking **Rook.**
[roək.]

No smoking **Rook verbode.**
[roək ferbodə.]

Excuse me! (addressing a waiter) **Hallo! Verskoning!**
[hallo! ferskoniŋ!]

menu **spyskaart**
[spajskärt]

wine list **wynkaart**
[vajn·kärt]

The menu, please. **Die spyskaart, asseblief.**
[di spajskärt, asseblif.]

Are you ready to order? **Is u gereed om te bestel?**
[is u χereət om tə bestel?]

What will you have? **Wat verkies u?**
[vat ferkis u?]

I'll have ... **Ek wil ... hê**
[ɛk vil ... hɛ:]

I'm a vegetarian. **Ek is vegetariër**
[ɛk is feχetariɛr]

meat **vleis**
[flæjs]

fish **vis**
[fis]

vegetables **groente**
[χruntə]

Do you have vegetarian dishes? **Het u vegetariese geregte?**
[het u feχetarisə χereχtə?]

I don't eat pork. **Ek eet nie varkvleis nie.**
[ɛk eət ni fark·flæjs ni.]

He /she/ doesn't eat meat. **Hy /sy/ eet nie vleis nie.**
[haj /saj/ eət ni flæjs ni.]

I am allergic to ... **Ek is allergies vir ...**
[ɛk is allerχis fir ...]

Would you please bring me ...	**Bring vir my ..., asseblief** [briŋ fir maj ..., asseblif]
salt | pepper | sugar	**sout | peper | suiker** [sæʊt | pepər | sœikər]
coffee | tea | dessert	**koffie | tee | nagereg** [koffi | teə | naχerəχ]
water | sparkling | plain	**water | bruisend | plat** [vatər | brœisent | plat]
a spoon | fork | knife	**'n lepel | vurk | mes** [ə lepəl | furk | mes]
a plate | napkin	**'n bord | servet** [ə bort | serfet]

Enjoy your meal!	**Smaaklike ete!** [smāklikə ete!]
One more, please.	**Nog een, asseblief.** [noχ eən, asseblif.]
It was very delicious.	**Dit was heerlik.** [dit vas heərlik.]

check | change | tip	**rekening | wisselgeld | fooitjie** [rekəniŋ | vissəlχɛlt | fojki]
Check, please. (Could I have the check, please?)	**Die rekening, asseblief.** [di rekəniŋ, asseblif.]
Can I pay by credit card?	**Kan ek met 'n kredietkaart betaal?** [kan ɛk met ə kreditkārt betāl?]
I'm sorry, there's a mistake here.	**Jammer, hier is 'n fout.** [jammər, hir is ə fæʊt.]

Shopping

Can I help you?
Kan ek help?
[kan ek hɛlp?]

Do you have ...?
Het u ...?
[het u ...?]

I'm looking for ...
Ek soek ...
[ɛk suk ...]

I need ...
Ek het ... nodig
[ɛk het ... nodəχ]

I'm just looking.
Ek kyk net.
[ɛk kajk net.]

We're just looking.
Ons kyk net.
[ɔŋs kajk net.]

I'll come back later.
Ek kom netnou terug.
[ɛk kom netnæʊ teruχ.]

We'll come back later.
Ons kom netnou terug.
[ɔŋs kom netnæʊ teruχ.]

discounts | sale
afslag | uitverkoping
[afslaχ | œitferkopiŋ]

Would you please show me ...
Kan u my ... wys, asseblief?
[kan u maj ... vajs, asseblif?]

Would you please give me ...
Kan u my ... gee, asseblief?
[kan u maj ... χeə, asseblif?]

Can I try it on?
Kan ek dit aanpas?
[kan ɛk dit ānpas?]

Excuse me, where's the fitting room?
Verskoon tog, waar is die paskamer?
[ferskoən toχ, vār is di paskamer?]

Which color would you like?
Watter kleur wil u hê?
[vattər kløər vil u hɛ:?]

size | length
maat | lengte
[māt | leŋtə]

How does it fit?
Pas dit?
[pas dit?]

How much is it?
Hoeveel kos dit?
[hufeəl kos dit?]

That's too expensive.
Dis te duur
[dis tə dɪr]

I'll take it.
Ek sal dit vat.
[ɛk sal dit fat.]

Excuse me, where do I pay?
Verskoon tog, waar moet ek betaal?
[ferskoən toχ, vār mut ek betāl?]

Will you pay in cash or credit card?	**Betaal u kontant of met 'n kredietkaart?** [betal u kontant of met ə kreditkãrt?]
In cash | with credit card	**kontant | met 'n kredietkaart** [kontant | met ə kreditkãrt]

Do you want the receipt?	**Wil u 'n ontvangsbewys?** [vil u ə ontfaŋsbevajs?]
Yes, please.	**Ja, asseblief.** [ja, asseblif.]
No, it's OK.	**Nee, dis nie nodig nie.** [neə, dis ni nodəχ ni.]
Thank you. Have a nice day!	**Dankie. Geniet die res van die dag!** [danki. χenit di res fan di daχ!]

In town

Excuse me, please.	**Verskoon tog, asseblief.** [ferskoən toχ, asseblif.]
I'm looking for …	**Ek soek …** [ɛk suk …]
the subway	**die moltrein** [di moltræjn]
my hotel	**my hotel** [maj hotəl]
the movie theater	**die bioskoop** [di bioskoəp]
a taxi stand	**'n taxistaanplek** [ə taksi·stānplek]
an ATM	**'n OTM** [ə o·te·em]
a foreign exchange office	**'n wisselkantoor** [ə vissəl·kantoər]
an internet café	**'n internetkafee** [ə internet·kafeə]
… street	**… straat** [… strāt]
this place	**hierdie plek** [hirdi plek]
Do you know where … is?	**Weet u waar … is?** [veət u vār … is?]
Which street is this?	**Watter straat is dit?** [vattər strāt is dit?]
Show me where we are right now.	**Kan u my aanwys waar ons nou is?** [kan u maj ānwajs vār ɔŋs næʊ is?]
Can I get there on foot?	**Kan ek soontoe stap?** [kan ek soentu stap?]
Do you have a map of the city?	**Het u 'n kaart van die stad?** [het u ə kārt fan di stat?]
How much is a ticket to get in?	**Hoeveel kos 'n toegangskaartjie?** [hufeəl kos ə tuχaŋs·kārki?]
Can I take pictures here?	**Kan ek hier foto's maak?** [kan ɛk hir fotos māk?]
Are you open?	**Is u oop?** [is u oəp?]

When do you open?

Hoe laat gaan u oop?
[hu lāt χãn u oəp?]

When do you close?

Hoe laat sluit u?
[hu lāt slœit u?]

Money

money	**geld** [χɛlt]
cash	**kontant** [kontant]
paper money	**bankbiljette** [bank·biljɛttə]
loose change	**kleingeld** [klæjn·χɛlt]
check | change | tip	**rekening | wisselgeld | fooitjie** [rekəniŋ | vissəlχɛlt | fojki]
credit card	**kredietkaart** [kreditkārt]
wallet	**beursie** [bøərsi]
to buy	**koop** [koəp]
to pay	**betaal** [betāl]
fine	**boete** [butə]
free	**gratis** [χratis]
Where can I buy ...?	**Waar kan ek ... koop?** [vār kan ɛk ... koəp?]
Is the bank open now?	**Is die bank nou oop?** [is di bank næʊ oəp?]
When does it open?	**Wanneer maak dit oop?** [vanneər māk dit oəp?]
When does it close?	**Wanneer maak dit toe?** [vanneər māk dit tu?]
How much?	**Hoeveel?** [hufeəl?]
How much is this?	**Hoeveel kos dit?** [hufeəl kos dit?]
That's too expensive.	**Dis te duur.** [dis tə dɪr.]
Excuse me, where do I pay?	**Verskoon tog, waar moet ek betaal?** [ferskoən toχ, vār mut ek betāl?]
Check, please.	**Die rekening, asseblief.** [di rekəniŋ, asseblif.]

Can I pay by credit card?

Kan ek met 'n kredietkaart betaal?
[kan ɛk met ə kreditkãrt betãl?]

Is there an ATM here?

Verskoon tog, is hier 'n OTM?
[ferskoən toχ, is hir ə o·te·em?]

I'm looking for an ATM.

Ek soek 'n OTM.
[ɛk suk ə o·te·em.]

I'm looking for a foreign exchange office.

Ek soek 'n wisselkantoor.
[ɛk suk ə vissəl·kantoər.]

I'd like to change ...

Ek sou ... wou wissel.
[ɛk sæʊ ... væʊ vissəl.]

What is the exchange rate?

Wat is die wisselkoers?
[vat is di vissəlkurs?]

Do you need my passport?

Het u my paspoort nodig?
[het u maj paspoərt nodəχ?]

Time

What time is it?	**Hoe laat is dit?** [hu lāt is dit?]
When?	**Wanneer?** [vanneər?]
At what time?	**Hoe laat?** [hu lāt?]
now | later | after ...	**nou | later | na ...** [næʊ | latər | na ...]
one o'clock	**een uur** [eən ɪr]
one fifteen	**kwart oor een** [kwart oər eən]
one thirty	**half twee** [half tweə]
one forty-five	**kwart voor twee** [kwart foər tweə]
one | two | three	**een | twee | drie** [eən | tweə | dri]
four | five | six	**vier | vyf | ses** [fir | fajf | ses]
seven | eight | nine	**sewe | ag | nege** [sevə | aχ | neχə]
ten | eleven | twelve	**tien | elf | twaalf** [tin | ɛlf | twālf]
in ...	**binne ...** [binnə ...]
five minutes	**vyf minute** [fajf minutə]
ten minutes	**tien minute** [tin minutə]
fifteen minutes	**vyftien minute** [fajftin minutə]
twenty minutes	**twintig minute** [twintəχ minutə]
half an hour	**'n halfuur** [ə halfɪr]
an hour	**'n uur** [ə ɪr]

in the morning | **soggens**
[soχεηs]

early in the morning | **soggens vroeg**
[soχεηs fruχ]

this morning | **vanoggend**
[fanoχent]

tomorrow morning | **môreoggend**
[mɔrǝ·oχent]

---

in the middle of the day | **in die middel van die dag**
[in di middǝl fan di daχ]

in the afternoon | **smiddags**
[smiddaχs]

in the evening | **saans**
[sãηs]

tonight | **vanaand**
[fanãnt]

---

at night | **saans**
[sãηs]

yesterday | **gister**
[χistǝr]

today | **vandag**
[fandaχ]

tomorrow | **môre**
[mɔrǝ]

the day after tomorrow | **oormôre**
[oǝrmɔrǝ]

What day is it today? | **Watter dag is dit vandag?**
[vattǝr daχ is dit fandaχ?]

It's … | **Dit is …**
[dit is …]

Monday | **maandag**
[mãndaχ]

Tuesday | **dinsdag**
[dinsdaχ]

Wednesday | **woensdag**
[voεηsdaχ]

Thursday | **Donderdag**
[dondǝrdaχ]

Friday | **vrydag**
[frajdaχ]

Saturday | **saterdag**
[satǝrdaχ]

Sunday | **sondag**
[sondaχ]

Greetings. Introductions

Hello.	**Hallo.** [hallo.]
Pleased to meet you.	**Aangename kennis.** [ãnχənamə kɛnnis.]
Me too.	**Dieselfde.** [disɛlfdə.]
I'd like you to meet …	**Kan ek jou voorstel aan …** [kan ɛk jæʊ foərstəl ãn …]
Nice to meet you.	**Aangename kennis.** [ãnχənamə kɛnnis.]

How are you?	**Hoe gaan dit?** [hu χãn dit?]
My name is …	**My naam is …** [maj nãm is …]
His name is …	**Dis …** [dis …]
Her name is …	**Dis …** [dis …]
What's your name?	**Wat is u naam?** [vat is u nãm?]
What's his name?	**Wat is sy naam?** [vat is saj nãm?]
What's her name?	**Wat is haar naam?** [vat is hãr nãm?]

What's your last name?	**Wat is u van?** [vat is u fan?]
You can call me …	**Noem my maar …** [num maj mãr …]
Where are you from?	**Vanwaar kom u?** [fanwãr kom u?]
I'm from …	**Ek kom van …** [ɛk kom fan …]
What do you do for a living?	**Wat is u beroep?** [vat is u berup?]
Who is this?	**Wie is dit?** [vi is dit?]
Who is he?	**Wie is hy?** [vi is haj?]
Who is she?	**Wie is sy?** [vi is saj?]
Who are they?	**Wie is hulle?** [vi is hullə?]

This is …	**Dit is …** [dit is …]
my friend (masc.)	**my vriend** [maj frint]
my friend (fem.)	**my vriendin** [maj frindin]
my husband	**my man** [maj man]
my wife	**my vrou** [maj fræʊ]

my father	**my vader** [maj fadər]
my mother	**my moeder** [maj mudər]
my brother	**my broer** [maj brur]
my son	**my seun** [maj søən]
my daughter	**my dogter** [maj doχtər]

This is our son.	**Dit is ons seun.** [dit is ɔŋs søən.]
This is our daughter.	**Dit is ons dogter.** [dit is ɔŋs doχter.]
These are my children.	**Dit is my kinders.** [dit is maj kindərs.]
These are our children.	**Dit is ons kinders.** [dit is ɔŋs kindərs.]

Farewells

Good bye!	**Totsiens!** [totsiŋs!]
Bye! (inform.)	**Koebaai!** [kubāi!]
See you tomorrow.	**Sien jou môre.** [sin jæʊ mɔrə.]
See you soon.	**Totsiens.** [totsiŋs.]
See you at seven.	**Sien jou om sewe uur.** [sin jæʊ om seve ɪr.]
Have fun!	**Geniet dit!** [χenit dit!]
Talk to you later.	**Gesels later.** [χesɛls latər.]
Have a nice weekend.	**Geniet die naweek.** [χenit di naveek.]
Good night.	**Lekker slaap.** [lɛkkər slāp.]
It's time for me to go.	**Dis tyd om te gaan.** [dis tajt om tə χān.]
I have to go.	**Ek moet loop.** [ɛk mut loəp.]
I will be right back.	**Ek is nounou terug.** [ɛk is næʊnæʊ teruχ.]
It's late.	**Dis al laat.** [dis al lāt.]
I have to get up early.	**Ek moet vroeg opstaan.** [ɛk mut fruχ opstān.]
I'm leaving tomorrow.	**Ek vertrek môre.** [ɛk fertrək mɔrə.]
We're leaving tomorrow.	**Ons vertrek môre.** [ɔŋs fertrek mɔrə.]
Have a nice trip!	**Geniet die reis!** [χenit di ræjs!]
It was nice meeting you.	**Ek het dit geniet om jou te ontmoet.** [ɛk het dit χenit om jæʊ tə ontmut.]
It was nice talking to you.	**Dit was lekker om met jou te gesels.** [dit vas lɛkkər om met jæʊ tə χesɛls.]
Thanks for everything.	**Baie dankie vir alles.** [baje danki fir alles.]

I had a very good time.

Ek het dit geniet.
[ɛk het dit χenit.]

We had a very good time.

Ons het dit baie geniet.
[ɔŋs het dit baje χenit.]

It was really great.

Dit was regtig oulik.
[dit vas reχtəχ æulik.]

I'm going to miss you.

Ek gaan jou mis.
[ɛk χān jæu mis.]

We're going to miss you.

Ons gaan jou mis.
[ɔŋs χān jæu mis.]

Good luck!

Sukses!
[suksɛs!]

Say hi to ...

Stuur groete vir ...
[stɪr χrutə fir ...]

Foreign language

I don't understand.	**Ek verstaan dit nie.** [ɛk ferstãn dit ni.]
Write it down, please.	**Skryf dit neer, asseblief.** [skrajf dit neer, asseblif.]
Do you speak …?	**Praat u …?** [prãt u …?]

I speak a little bit of …	**Ek praat 'n bietjie …** [ɛk prãt ə biki …]
English	**Engels** [ɛŋəls]
Turkish	**Turks** [turks]
Arabic	**Arabies** [arabis]
French	**Frans** [fraŋs]

German	**Duits** [dœits]
Italian	**Italiaans** [italiãŋs]
Spanish	**Spaans** [spãŋs]
Portuguese	**Portugees** [portuχeəs]
Chinese	**Sjinees** [ʃineəs]
Japanese	**Japannees** [japanneəs]

Can you repeat that, please.	**Kan u dit herhaal asseblief** [kan u dit herhãl asseblif]
I understand.	**Ek verstaan dit.** [ɛk ferstãn dit.]
I don't understand.	**Ek verstaan dit nie.** [ɛk ferstãn dit ni.]
Please speak more slowly.	**Praat bietjie stadiger asseblief.** [prãt biki stadiχər asseblif.]

Is that correct? (Am I saying it right?)	**Is dit reg?** [is dit reχ?]
What is this? (What does this mean?)	**Wat is dit?** [vat is dit?]

Apologies

Excuse me, please.	**Verskoon my, asseblief.** [fɛrskoən maj, assɛblif.]
I'm sorry.	**Jammer.** [jammər.]
I'm really sorry.	**Ek is baie jammer.** [ɛk is baje jammər.]
Sorry, it's my fault.	**Jammer, dis my skuld.** [jammər, dis maj skult.]
My mistake.	**My skuld.** [maj skult.]
May I ...?	**Mag ek ...?** [maχ ek ...?]
Do you mind if I ...?	**Sal u omgee as ek ...?** [sal u omχeə as ek ...?]
It's OK.	**Dis OK.** [dis okej.]
It's all right.	**Maak nie saak nie.** [māk ni sāk ni.]
Don't worry about it.	**Moet jou nie daaroor bekommer nie.** [mut jæʊ ni dāroər bekommər ni.]

Agreement

Yes.	**Ja.** [ja.]
Yes, sure.	**Ja, beslis.** [ja, beslis.]
OK (Good!)	**OK. Goed!** [okej. χut!]
Very well.	**Uitstekend.** [œitstekent]
Certainly!	**Definitief!** [definitif!]
I agree.	**Ek stem saam.** [ɛk stem sãm.]
That's correct.	**Dis reg.** [dis reχ.]
That's right.	**Dis reg.** [dis reχ.]
You're right.	**U is reg.** [u is reχ.]
I don't mind.	**Ek gee nie om nie.** [ɛk χeə ni om ni.]
Absolutely right.	**Heeltemal reg.** [heəltemal reχ.]
It's possible.	**Dis moontlik.** [dis moentlik.]
That's a good idea.	**Dis 'n goeie idee.** [dis ə χuje ideə.]
I can't say no.	**Ek kan nie nee sê nie.** [ɛk kan ni neə sɛ: ni.]
I'd be happy to.	**Dis 'n plesier.** [dis ə plesir.]
With pleasure.	**Plesier.** [plesir.]

Refusal. Expressing doubt

No.	**Nee** [neə]
Certainly not.	**Beslis nie.** [beslis ni.]
I don't agree.	**Ek stem nie saam nie.** [ɛk stem ni sãm ni.]
I don't think so.	**Ek glo dit nie.** [ɛk χlo dit ni.]
It's not true.	**Dis nie waar nie.** [dis ni vãr ni.]
You are wrong.	**U maak 'n fout.** [u mãk ə fæʊt.]
I think you are wrong.	**Ek dink u is verkeerd.** [ɛk dink u is ferkeərt.]
I'm not sure.	**Ek is nie seker nie.** [ɛk is ni sekər ni.]
It's impossible.	**Dis onmoontlik.** [dis onmoentlik.]
Nothing of the kind (sort)!	**Glad nie!** [χlat ni!]
The exact opposite.	**Net die teenoorgestelde!** [net di teənoərχestɛlde!]
I'm against it.	**Ek is daarteen.** [ɛk is dãrteən.]
I don't care.	**Ek gee nie om nie.** [ɛk χeə ni om ni.]
I have no idea.	**Ek het nie 'n idee nie.** [ɛk het ni ə ideə ni.]
I doubt it.	**Ek betwyfel dit.** [ɛk betwajfəl dit.]
Sorry, I can't.	**Jammer, ek kan nie.** [jammər, ɛk kan ni.]
Sorry, I don't want to.	**Jammer, ek wil nie.** [jammər, ɛk vil ni.]
Thank you, but I don't need this.	**Dankie, maar ek het dit nie nodig nie.** [danki, mãr ɛk het dit ni nodəχ ni.]
It's getting late.	**Dit word laat.** [dit vort lãt.]

I have to get up early. **Ek moet vroeg opstaan.**
[ɛk mut fruχ opstãn.]

I don't feel well. **Ek voel nie lekker nie.**
[ɛk ful ni lɛkkər ni.]

Expressing gratitude

Thank you.	**Baie dankie.** [baje danki.]
Thank you very much.	**Baie dankie.** [baje danki.]
I really appreciate it.	**Ek waardeer dit.** [ɛk vãrdeǝr dit.]
I'm really grateful to you.	**Ek is u baie dankbaar.** [ɛk is u baje dankbãr.]
We are really grateful to you.	**Ons is u baie dankbaar.** [ɔŋs is u baje dankbãr.]
Thank you for your time.	**Baie dankie vir u tyd.** [baje danki fir u tajt.]
Thanks for everything.	**Baie dankie vir alles.** [baje danki fir alles.]
Thank you for ...	**Dankie vir ...** [danki fir ...]
your help	**u hulp** [u hulp]
a nice time	**vir 'n lekker tydjie** [fir ǝ lɛkkǝr tajʤi]
a wonderful meal	**'n heerlike ete** [ǝ heǝrlikǝ etǝ]
a pleasant evening	**'n aangename aand** [ǝ ãnχǝnamǝ ãnt]
a wonderful day	**'n oulike dag** [ǝ æʊlikǝ daχ]
an amazing journey	**'n wonderlike reis** [ǝ vondǝrlikǝ ræjs]
Don't mention it.	**Plesier.** [plesir.]
You are welcome.	**Plesier.** [plesir.]
Any time.	**Enige tyd.** [ɛniχǝ tajt.]
My pleasure.	**Plesier.** [plesir.]
Forget it.	**Plesier.** [plesir.]
Don't worry about it.	**Moet jou nie bekommer nie.** [mut jæʊ ni bekommǝr ni.]

Congratulations. Best wishes

Congratulations!	**Geluk!** [χeluk!]
Happy birthday!	**Geluk met jou verjaardag!** [χeluk met jæʊ ferjȧrdaχ!]
Merry Christmas!	**Geseënde Kersfees!** [χeseɛndə kersfeɛs!]
Happy New Year!	**Gelukkige Nuwejaar!** [χelukkiχə nuvejȧr!]
Happy Easter!	**Geseënde Paasfees!** [χeseɛndə pȧsfeɛs!]
Happy Hanukkah!	**Gelukkige Chanoeka!** [χelukkiχə χanuka!]
I'd like to propose a toast.	**Ek wil graag 'n heildronk instel.** [ɛk vil χrȧχ ə hæjldronk instəl.]
Cheers!	**Gesondheid!** [χesonthæjt!]
Let's drink to …!	**Laat ons drink op …!** [lȧt ɔŋs drink op …!]
To our success!	**Op jou sukses!** [op jæʊ suksɛs!]
To your success!	**Op u sukses!** [op u suksɛs!]
Good luck!	**Sukses!** [suksɛs!]
Have a nice day!	**Geniet die dag!** [χenit di daχ!]
Have a good holiday!	**Geniet die vakansie!** [χenit di fakaŋsi!]
Have a safe journey!	**Veilig ry!** [fæjləχ raj!]
I hope you get better soon!	**Ek hoop u voel gou beter!** [ɛk hoəp u ful χæʊ betər!]

Socializing

Why are you sad?	**Hoekom lyk u so droewig?** [hukom lajk u so druvəχ?]
Smile! Cheer up!	**Lag 'n bietjie! Wees vrolik!** [laχ ə biki! veəs frolik!]
Are you free tonight?	**Is u vry vanaand?** [is u fraj fanãnt?]
May I offer you a drink?	**Kan ek 'n drankie vir jou kry?** [kan ek ə dranki fir jæʊ kraj?]
Would you like to dance?	**Wil u dans?** [vil u daŋs?]
Let's go to the movies.	**Sal ons bioskoop toe gaan?** [sal ɔŋs bioskoəp tu χãn?]
May I invite you to ...?	**Mag ek jou uitnooi na ...?** [maχ ek jæʊ œitnoj na ...?]
a restaurant	**'n restaurant** [ə restɔurant]
the movies	**die bioskoop** [di bioskoəp]
the theater	**die teater** [di teatər]
go for a walk	**gaan stap** [χãn stap]
At what time?	**Hoe laat?** [hu lãt?]
tonight	**vanaand** [fanãnt]
at six	**om ses uur** [om sɛs ɪr]
at seven	**om sewe uur** [om sevə ɪr]
at eight	**om agt uur** [om aχt ɪr]
at nine	**om nege uur** [om neχə ɪr]
Do you like it here?	**Geniet u dit hier?** [χenit u dit hir?]
Are you here with someone?	**Is u hier saam met iemand?** [is u hir sãm met imant?]
I'm with my friend.	**Ek is met my vriend.** [ɛk is met maj frint.]

I'm with my friends.

Ek is met my vriende.
[ɛk is met maj frində.]

No, I'm alone.

Nee, ek is alleen.
[neə, ek is alleʊn.]

Do you have a boyfriend?

Het jy 'n kêrel?
[het jaj ə kærel?]

I have a boyfriend.

Ek het 'n kêrel.
[ɛk het ə kærel.]

Do you have a girlfriend?

Het jy 'n meisie?
[het jaj ə mæjsi?]

I have a girlfriend.

Ek het 'n meisie.
[ɛk het ə mæjsi.]

Can I see you again?

Kan ek jou weer sien?
[kan ek jæʊ veər sin?]

Can I call you?

Kan ek jou bel?
[kan ek jæʊ bel?]

Call me. (Give me a call.)

Bel my.
[bel maj.]

What's your number?

Wat is jou nommer?
[vat is jæʊ nommər?]

I miss you.

Ek mis jou.
[ɛk mis jæʊ.]

You have a beautiful name.

U het 'n mooi naam.
[u het ə moj nãm.]

I love you.

Ek hou van jou.
[ɛk hæʊ fan jæʊ.]

Will you marry me?

Wil jy met my trou?
[vil jaj met maj træʊ?]

You're kidding!

U maak grappies!
[u mãk χrappis!]

I'm just kidding.

Ek maak net 'n grappie.
[ɛk mãk net ə χrappi.]

Are you serious?

Bedoel u dit?
[bedul u dit?]

I'm serious.

Ek is ernstig.
[ɛk is ernstəχ.]

Really?!

Regtig waar?!
[reχtəχ vãr?!]

It's unbelievable!

Dis ongelooflik.
[dis onχeloəflik.]

I don't believe you.

Ek glo jou nie.
[ɛk χlo jæʊ ni.]

I can't.

Ek kan nie.
[ɛk kan ni.]

I don't know.

Ek weet dit nie.
[ɛk veət dit ni.]

I don't understand you.

Ek verstaan u nie.
[ɛk ferstãn u ni.]

Please go away.

Loop asseblief.
[loəp asseblif.]

Leave me alone!

Los my uit!
[los maj œit!]

I can't stand him.

Ek kan hom nie verdra nie.
[ɛk kan hom ni ferdra ni.]

You are disgusting!

U is walglik!
[u is valχlik!]

I'll call the police!

Ek gaan die polisie bel!
[ɛk χān di polisi bel!]

Sharing impressions. Emotions

I like it.	**Ek hou daarvan.** [ɛk hæʊ dārfan.]
Very nice.	**Baie mooi.** [baje moj.]
That's great!	**Dis oulik!** [dis æʊlik!]
It's not bad.	**Dis nie sleg nie.** [dis ni sleχ ni.]
I don't like it.	**Ek hou nie daarvan nie.** [ɛk hæʊ ni dārfan ni.]
It's not good.	**Dis nie goed nie.** [dis ni χut ni.]
It's bad.	**Dis sleg.** [dis sleχ.]
It's very bad.	**Dis baie sleg.** [dis baje sleχ.]
It's disgusting.	**Dis walglik.** [dis valχlik.]
I'm happy.	**Ek is bly.** [ɛk is blaj.]
I'm content.	**Ek is tevrede.** [ɛk is tefrede.]
I'm in love.	**Ek is verlief.** [ɛk is ferlif.]
I'm calm.	**Ek is rustig.** [ɛk is rustəχ.]
I'm bored.	**Ek verveel my.** [ɛk ferfeəl maj.]
I'm tired.	**Ek is moeg.** [ɛk is muχ.]
I'm sad.	**Ek is droewig.** [ɛk is druvəχ.]
I'm frightened.	**Ek is bang.** [ɛk is baŋ.]
I'm angry.	**Ek is kwaad.** [ɛk is kwāt.]
I'm worried.	**Ek is bekommerd.** [ɛk is bekommert.]
I'm nervous.	**Ek is senuweeagtig.** [ɛk is senuveə aχtəχ.]

I'm jealous. (envious)

Ek is jaloers.
[ɛk is jalurs.]

I'm surprised.

Dit verbaas my.
[dit ferbãs maj.]

I'm perplexed.

Ek is verbouereerd.
[ɛk is ferbæʊreert.]

Problems. Accidents

I've got a problem. | **Ek het 'n probleem.**
[ɛk het ə probleəm.]

We've got a problem. | **Ons het 'n probleem.**
[ɔŋs het ə probleəm.]

I'm lost. | **Ek het verdwaal.**
[ɛk het ferdwāl.]

I missed the last bus (train). | **Ek het die laaste bus (trein) gemis.**
[ɛk het di lāstə bus (træjn) χemis.]

I don't have any money left. | **My geld is op.**
[maj χɛlt is op.]

I've lost my … | **Ek het my … verloor**
[ɛk het maj … ferloər]

Someone stole my … | **Iemand het my … gesteel.**
[iemant het maj … χesteəl.]

passport | **paspoort**
[paspoərt]

wallet | **beursie**
[bøərsi]

papers | **papiere**
[papirə]

ticket | **kaartjie**
[kārki]

money | **geld**
[χɛlt]

handbag | **handsak**
[hand·sak]

camera | **kamera**
[kamera]

laptop | **skootrekenaar**
[skoət·rekənār]

tablet computer | **tablet**
[tablet]

mobile phone | **selfoon**
[sɛlfoən]

Help me! | **Help!**
[hɛlp!]

What's happened? | **Wat's fout?**
[vats fæʊt?]

fire | **brand**
[brant]

shooting	**daar word geskiet** [dãr vort χeskit]
murder	**moord** [moərt]
explosion	**ontploffing** [ontploffiŋ]
fight	**geveg** [χefeχ]

Call the police!	**Bel die polisie!** [bel di polisi!]
Please hurry up!	**Maak gou asseblief!** [mãk χæʊ asseblif!]
I'm looking for the police station.	**Ek soek die polisiekantoor.** [ɛk suk di polisi·kantoər.]
I need to make a call.	**Ek moet bel.** [ɛk mut bel.]
May I use your phone?	**Mag ek u telefoon gebruik?** [maχ ek u telefoən χebrœik?]

I've been …	**Ek is …** [ɛk is …]
mugged	**aangeval** [ãnχəfal]
robbed	**beroof** [beroəf]
raped	**verkrag** [ferkraχ]
attacked (beaten up)	**aangeval** [ãnχəfal]

Are you all right?	**Gaan dit?** [χãn dit?]
Did you see who it was?	**Het u gesien wie dit was?** [het u χesin vi dit vas?]
Would you be able to recognize the person?	**Sou u die persoon kon herken?** [sæʊ u di persoən kon herken?]
Are you sure?	**Is u seker?** [is u seker?]

Please calm down.	**Kom tot bedaring asseblief.** [kom tot bedariŋ asseblif.]
Take it easy!	**Rustig!** [rustəχ!]
Don't worry!	**Moenie bekommerd wees nie!** [muni bekommert veəs ni!]
Everything will be fine.	**Alles sal reg kom.** [alles sal reχ kom.]
Everything's all right.	**Alles is reg.** [alles is reχ.]
Come here, please.	**Kom hier asseblief.** [kom hir asseblif.]

I have some questions for you.

Ek het 'n paar vrae vir u.
[ɛk het ə pār fraə fir u.]

Wait a moment, please.

Wag 'n bietjie, asseblief.
[vaχ ə biki, asseblif.]

Do you have any I.D.?

Het u 'n identiteitskaart?
[het u ə identitæjts·kārt?]

Thanks. You can leave now.

Dankie. U kan nou loop.
[danki. u kan næʋ loəp.]

Hands behind your head!

Hande agter jou kop!
[handə aχtər jæʋ kop!]

You're under arrest!

U is onder arres!
[u is ondər arres!]

Health problems

Please help me.	**Help my, asseblief.** [hɛlp maj, asseblif.]
I don't feel well.	**Ek voel nie lekker nie.** [ɛk ful ni lɛkkər ni.]
My husband doesn't feel well.	**My man voel nie lekker nie.** [maj man ful ni lɛkkər ni.]
My son ...	**My seun ...** [maj søən ...]
My father ...	**My pa ...** [maj pa ...]
My wife doesn't feel well.	**My vrou voel nie lekker nie.** [maj fræʊ ful ni lɛkkər ni.]
My daughter ...	**My dogter ...** [maj doχtər ...]
My mother ...	**My ma ...** [maj ma ...]
I've got a ...	**Ek het ...** [ɛk het ...]
headache	**koppyn** [koppajn]
sore throat	**keelpyn** [keəl·pajn]
stomach ache	**maagpyn** [mãχpajn]
toothache	**tandpyn** [tand·pajn]
I feel dizzy.	**Ek voel duiselig.** [ɛk ful dœiseləχ.]
He has a fever.	**Hy het koors.** [haj het koərs.]
She has a fever.	**Sy het koors.** [saj het koərs.]
I can't breathe.	**Ek kan nie goed asemhaal nie.** [ɛk kan ni χut asemhãl ni.]
I'm short of breath.	**Ek is kortasem.** [ɛk is kortasem.]
I am asthmatic.	**Ek is asmaties.** [ɛk is asmatis.]
I am diabetic.	**Ek is diabeet.** [ɛk is diabeət.]

I can't sleep.

Ek kan nie slaap nie.
[ɛk kan ni slāp ni.]

food poisoning

voedselvergiftiging
[fudsəl·fɐrχiftəχiŋ]

It hurts here.

Dis seer hier.
[dis seər hir.]

Help me!

Help!
[hɛlp!]

I am here!

Ek is hier!
[ɛk is hir!]

We are here!

Ons is hier!
[oŋs is hir!]

Get me out of here!

Kom kry my!
[kom kraj maj!]

I need a doctor.

Ek het 'n dokter nodig.
[ɛk het ə doktər nodəχ.]

I can't move.

Ek kan nie beweeg nie.
[ɛk kan ni beveəχ ni.]

I can't move my legs.

Ek kan my bene nie beweeg nie.
[ɛk kan maj benə ni beveəχ ni.]

I have a wound.

Ek het 'n wond.
[ɛk het ə vont.]

Is it serious?

Is dit ernstig?
[is dit ernstəχ?]

My documents are in my pocket.

My dokumente is in my sak.
[maj dokumentə is in maj sak.]

Calm down!

Bedaar!
[bedār!]

May I use your phone?

Mag ek u telefoon gebruik?
[maχ ek u telefoən χebrœik?]

Call an ambulance!

Bel 'n ambulans!
[bel ə ambulaŋs!]

It's urgent!

Dis dringend!
[dis driŋənd!]

It's an emergency!

Dis 'n noodgeval!
[dis ə noədχefal!]

Please hurry up!

Maak gou asseblief!
[māk χæʊ asseblif!]

Would you please call a doctor?

Kan u asseblief 'n dokter bel?
[kan u asseblif ə doktər bel?]

Where is the hospital?

Waar is die hospitaal?
[vār is di hospitāl?]

How are you feeling?

Hoe voel u?
[hu ful u?]

Are you all right?

Hoe gaan dit?
[hu χān dit?]

What's happened?

Wat het gebeur?
[vat het χebøər?]

I feel better now.	**Ek voel nou beter.** [ɛk ful næʊ betər.]
It's OK.	**Dis OK.** [dis okej.]
It's all right.	**Dit gaan goed.** [dit χān χut.]

At the pharmacy

pharmacy (drugstore)	**apteek** [apteək]
24-hour pharmacy	**24 uur apteek** [fir-en-twintəχ ɪr apteək]
Where is the closest pharmacy?	**Waar is die naaste apteek?** [vãr is di nãstə apteək?]

Is it open now?	**Is hy nou oop?** [is haj næʊ oəp?]
At what time does it open?	**Hoe laat gaan hy oop?** [hu lãt χãn haj oəp?]
At what time does it close?	**Hoe laat sluit hy?** [hu lãt slœit haj?]

Is it far?	**Is dit ver?** [is dit fer?]
Can I get there on foot?	**Kan ek soontoe stap?** [kan ek soentu stap?]
Can you show me on the map?	**Kan u dit op die stadskaart aanwys?** [kan u dit op di statskãrt ãnwajs?]

Please give me something for ...	**Gee my iets vir ... asseblief** [χeə maj its fir ... asseblif]
a headache	**koppyn** [koppajn]
a cough	**hoes** [hus]
a cold	**verkoudheid** [ferkæʊdhæjt]
the flu	**griep** [χrip]

a fever	**koors** [koərs]
a stomach ache	**maagpyn** [mãχpajn]
nausea	**naarheid** [nãrhæjt]
diarrhea	**diarree** [diarreə]
constipation	**konstipasie** [koŋstipasi]
pain in the back	**rugpyn** [ruχpajn]

chest pain	**borspyn** [borspajn]
side stitch	**steek in my sy** [steək in maj saj]
abdominal pain	**pyn in my onderbuik** [pajn in maj ondərbœik]

pill	**pil** [pil]
ointment, cream	**salf, room** [salf, roəm]
syrup	**stroop** [stroəp]
spray	**sproeier** [sprujer]
drops	**druppels** [druppɛls]

You need to go to the hospital.	**U moet hospitaal toe gaan.** [u mut hospitāl tu χān.]
health insurance	**siekteversekering** [siktə·fersekeriŋ]
prescription	**voorskrif** [foərskrif]
insect repellant	**insekmiddel** [insek·middəl]
Band Aid	**kleefverband** [kleəffər·bant]

The bare minimum

Excuse me, ...	**Verskoon my, ...** [ferskoən maj, ...]
Hello.	**Hallo.** [hallo.]
Thank you.	**Baie dankie.** [baje danki.]
Good bye.	**Totsiens.** [totsiŋs.]
Yes.	**Ja.** [ja.]
No.	**Nee.** [neə.]
I don't know.	**Ek weet nie.** [ɛk veət ni.]
Where?	Where to?	When?	**Waar?	Waarheen?	Wanneer?** [vãr?	vãrheən?	vanneər?]

I need ...	**Ek het ... nodig** [ɛk het ... nodəχ]
I want ...	**Ek wil ...** [ɛk vil ...]
Do you have ...?	**Het u ...?** [het u ...?]
Is there a ... here?	**Is hier 'n ...?** [is hir ə ...?]
May I ...?	**Mag ek ...?** [maχ ek ...?]
..., please (polite request)	**... asseblief** [... asseblif]

I'm looking for ...	**Ek soek ...** [ɛk suk ...]
restroom	**toilet** [tojlet]
ATM	**OTM** [o·te·em]
pharmacy (drugstore)	**apteek** [apteək]
hospital	**hospitaal** [hospitãl]
police station	**polisiekantoor** [polisi·kantoər]
subway	**moltrein** [moltræjn]

taxi	**taxi** [taksi]
train station	**stasie** [stasi]

My name is ...	**My naam is …** [maj nãm is …]
What's your name?	**Wat is u naam?** [vat is u nãm?]
Could you please help me?	**Kan u my help, asseblief?** [kan u maj hɛlp, asseblif?]
I've got a problem.	**Ek het 'n probleem.** [ɛk het ə probleəm.]
I don't feel well.	**Ek voel nie lekker nie.** [ɛk ful ni lɛkkər ni.]
Call an ambulance!	**Bel 'n ambulans!** [bel ə ambulaŋs!]
May I make a call?	**Kan ek 'n oproep maak?** [kan ɛk ə oprup mãk?]

I'm sorry.	**Jammer.** [jammər.]
You're welcome.	**Plesier.** [plesir.]

I, me	**Ek, my** [ek, maj]
you (inform.)	**jy** [jaj]
he	**hy** [haj]
she	**sy** [saj]
they (masc.)	**hulle** [hullə]
they (fem.)	**hulle** [hullə]
we	**ons** [ɔŋs]
you (pl)	**julle** [jullə]
you (sg, form.)	**u** [u]

ENTRANCE	**INGANG** [inχaŋ]
EXIT	**UITGANG** [œitχaŋ]
OUT OF ORDER	**BUITE WERKING** [bœitə verkiŋ]
CLOSED	**GESLUIT** [χeslœit]

OPEN	**OOP**
	[oəp]
FOR WOMEN	**DAMES**
	[dames]
FOR MEN	**MANS**
	[maŋs]

CONCISE DICTIONARY

This section contains more than 1,500 useful words arranged alphabetically. The dictionary includes a lot of gastronomic terms and will be helpful when ordering food at a restaurant or buying groceries

T&P Books Publishing

DICTIONARY CONTENTS

T&P Books Publishing

T&P Books Publishing

time	**tyd**	[tajt]
hour	**uur**	[ɪr]
half an hour	**n halfuur**	[n halfɪr]
minute	**minuut**	[minɪt]
second	**sekonde**	[sekondə]

today (adv)	**vandag**	[fandaχ]
tomorrow (adv)	**môre**	[mɔrə]
yesterday (adv)	**gister**	[χistər]

Monday	**Maandag**	[mãndaχ]
Tuesday	**Dinsdag**	[dinsdaχ]
Wednesday	**Woensdag**	[voɛŋsdaχ]
Thursday	**Donderdag**	[dondərdaχ]
Friday	**Vrydag**	[frajdaχ]
Saturday	**Saterdag**	[satərdaχ]
Sunday	**Sondag**	[sondaχ]

day	**dag**	[daχ]
working day	**werksdag**	[verks·daχ]
public holiday	**openbare vakansiedag**	[openbarə fakaŋsi·daχ]
weekend	**naweek**	[naveək]

week	**week**	[veək]
last week (adv)	**laas week**	[lãs veək]
next week (adv)	**volgende week**	[folχendə veək]

| sunrise | **sonop** | [son·op] |
| sunset | **sononder** | [son·ondər] |

| in the morning | **soggens** | [soχɛŋs] |
| in the afternoon | **in die namiddag** | [in di namiddaχ] |

| in the evening | **saans** | [sãŋs] |
| tonight (this evening) | **vanaand** | [fanãnt] |

| at night | **snags** | [snaχs] |
| midnight | **middernag** | [middərnaχ] |

January	**Januarie**	[januari]
February	**Februarie**	[februari]
March	**Maart**	[mãrt]
April	**April**	[april]
May	**Mei**	[mæj]
June	**Junie**	[juni]

July	**Julie**	[juli]
August	**Augustus**	[ɔuχustus]
September	**September**	[september]
October	**Oktober**	[oktober]
November	**November**	[nofember]
December	**Desember**	[desember]

in spring	**in die lente**	[in di lente]
in summer	**in die somer**	[in di somer]
in fall	**in die herfs**	[in di herfs]
in winter	**in die winter**	[in di vinter]

month	**maand**	[mānt]
season (summer, etc.)	**seisoen**	[sæjsun]
year	**jaar**	[jār]
century	**eeu**	[iʊ]

2. Numbers. Numerals

digit, figure	**syfer**	[sajfer]
number	**nommer**	[nommer]
minus sign	**minusteken**	[minus·teken]
plus sign	**plusteken**	[plus·teken]
sum, total	**som, totaal**	[som], [totāl]

first (adj)	**eerste**	[eerste]
second (adj)	**tweede**	[tweede]
third (adj)	**derde**	[derde]

0 zero	**nul**	[nul]
1 one	**een**	[een]
2 two	**twee**	[twee]
3 three	**drie**	[dri]
4 four	**vier**	[fir]

5 five	**vyf**	[fajf]
6 six	**ses**	[ses]
7 seven	**sewe**	[seve]
8 eight	**ag**	[aχ]
9 nine	**nege**	[neχe]
10 ten	**tien**	[tin]

11 eleven	**elf**	[ɛlf]
12 twelve	**twaalf**	[twālf]
13 thirteen	**dertien**	[dertin]
14 fourteen	**veertien**	[feertin]
15 fifteen	**vyftien**	[fajftin]

| 16 sixteen | **sestien** | [sestin] |
| 17 seventeen | **sewetien** | [sevetin] |

18 eighteen	agtien	[aχtin]
19 nineteen	negetien	[neχetin]
20 twenty	twintig	[twintəχ]
30 thirty	dertig	[dertəχ]
40 forty	veertig	[feərtəχ]
50 fifty	vyftig	[fajftəχ]
60 sixty	sestig	[sestəχ]
70 seventy	sewentig	[seventəχ]
80 eighty	tagtig	[taχtəχ]
90 ninety	negentig	[neχentəχ]
100 one hundred	honderd	[hondərt]
200 two hundred	tweehonderd	[twee·hondərt]
300 three hundred	driehonderd	[dri·hondərt]
400 four hundred	vierhonderd	[fir·hondərt]
500 five hundred	vyfhonderd	[fajf·hondərt]
600 six hundred	seshonderd	[ses·hondərt]
700 seven hundred	sewehonderd	[sevə·hondərt]
800 eight hundred	aghonderd	[aχ·hondərt]
900 nine hundred	negehonderd	[neχə·hondərt]
1000 one thousand	duisend	[dœisent]
10000 ten thousand	tienduisend	[tin·dœisent]
one hundred thousand	honderdduisend	[hondərt·dajsent]
million	miljoen	[miljun]
billion	miljard	[miljart]

3. Humans. Family

man (adult male)	man	[man]
young man	jongman	[joŋman]
teenager	tiener	[tinər]
woman	vrou	[fræʊ]
girl (young woman)	meisie	[mæjsi]
age	ouderdom	[æʊderdom]
adult (adj)	volwasse	[folwassə]
middle-aged (adj)	middeljarig	[middəl·jarəχ]
elderly (adj)	bejaard	[bejãrt]
old (adj)	oud	[æʊt]
old man	ou man	[æʊ man]
old woman	ou vrou	[æʊ fræʊ]
retirement	pensioen	[pɛnsiun]
to retire (from job)	met pensioen gaan	[met pɛnsiun χãn]
retiree	pensioenaris	[pɛnsiunaris]

mother	**moeder**	[mudər]
father	**vader**	[fadər]
son	**seun**	[søøn]
daughter	**dogter**	[doχtər]
brother	**broer**	[brur]
elder brother	**ouer broer**	[æʋer brur]
younger brother	**jonger broer**	[joŋər brur]
sister	**suster**	[sustər]
elder sister	**ouer suster**	[æʋer sustər]
younger sister	**jonger suster**	[joŋər sustər]
parents	**ouers**	[æʋers]
child	**kind**	[kint]
children	**kinders**	[kindərs]
stepmother	**stiefma**	[stifma]
stepfather	**stiefpa**	[stifpa]
grandmother	**ouma**	[æʋma]
grandfather	**oupa**	[æʋpa]
grandson	**kleinseun**	[klæjn·søøn]
granddaughter	**kleindogter**	[klæjn·doχtər]
grandchildren	**kleinkinders**	[klæjn·kindərs]
uncle	**oom**	[oəm]
aunt	**tante**	[tantə]
nephew	**neef**	[neəf]
niece	**nig**	[niχ]
wife	**vrou**	[fræʋ]
husband	**man**	[man]
married (masc.)	**getroud**	[χetræʋt]
married (fem.)	**getroud**	[χetræʋt]
widow	**weduwee**	[veduveə]
widower	**wedunaar**	[vedunãr]
name (first name)	**voornaam**	[foərnãm]
surname (last name)	**van**	[fan]
relative	**familielid**	[famililit]
friend (masc.)	**vriend**	[frint]
friendship	**vriendskap**	[frindskap]
partner	**maat**	[mãt]
superior (n)	**baas**	[bãs]
colleague	**kollega**	[kolleχa]
neighbors	**bure**	[burə]

4. Human body

organism (body)	**organisme**	[orχanismə]
body	**liggaam**	[liχχãm]

heart	**hart**	[hart]
blood	**bloed**	[blut]
brain	**brein**	[bræjn]
nerve	**senuwee**	[senuveə]
bone	**been**	[beən]
skeleton	**geraamte**	[χerãmtə]
spine (backbone)	**ruggraat**	[ruχ·χrãt]
rib	**rib**	[rip]
skull	**skedel**	[skedəl]
muscle	**spier**	[spir]
lungs	**longe**	[loŋə]
skin	**vel**	[fəl]
head	**kop**	[kop]
face	**gesig**	[χesəχ]
nose	**neus**	[nøəs]
forehead	**voorhoof**	[foərhoəf]
cheek	**wang**	[vaŋ]
mouth	**mond**	[mont]
tongue	**tong**	[toŋ]
tooth	**tand**	[tant]
lips	**lippe**	[lippə]
chin	**ken**	[ken]
ear	**oor**	[oər]
neck	**nek**	[nek]
throat	**keel**	[keəl]
eye	**oog**	[oəχ]
pupil	**pupil**	[pupil]
eyebrow	**wenkbrou**	[vɛnk·bræʊ]
eyelash	**ooghaar**	[oəχ·hãr]
hair	**haar**	[hãr]
hairstyle	**kapsel**	[kapsəl]
mustache	**snor**	[snor]
beard	**baard**	[bãrt]
to have (a beard, etc.)	**dra**	[dra]
bald (adj)	**kaal**	[kãl]
hand	**hand**	[hant]
arm	**arm**	[arm]
finger	**vinger**	[fiŋər]
nail	**nael**	[naəl]
palm	**palm**	[palm]
shoulder	**skouer**	[skæʊər]
leg	**been**	[beən]
foot	**voet**	[fut]

| knee | knie | [kni] |
| heel | hakskeen | [hak·skeən] |

back	rug	[ruχ]
waist	middel	[middəl]
beauty mark	moesie	[musi]
birthmark	moedervlek	[mudər·flek]
(café au lait spot)		

5. Medicine. Diseases. Drugs

health	gesondheid	[χesonthæjt]
well (not sick)	gesond	[χesont]
sickness	siekte	[siktə]
to be sick	siek wees	[sik veəs]
ill, sick (adj)	siek	[sik]

cold (illness)	verkoue	[ferkæʋə]
tonsillitis	keelontsteking	[keəl·ontstekiŋ]
pneumonia	longontsteking	[loŋ·ontstekiŋ]
flu, influenza	griep	[χrip]

runny nose (coryza)	loopneus	[loəpnøəs]
cough	hoes	[hus]
to cough (vi)	hoes	[hus]
to sneeze (vi)	nies	[nis]

stroke	beroerte	[berurtə]
heart attack	hartaanval	[hart·ānfal]
allergy	allergie	[allerχi]
asthma	asma	[asma]
diabetes	suikersiekte	[sœikər·siktə]

tumor	tumor	[tumor]
cancer	kanker	[kankər]
alcoholism	alkoholisme	[alkoholismə]
AIDS	VIGS	[vigs]
fever	koors	[koərs]
seasickness	seesiekte	[seə·siktə]

bruise (hématome)	blou kol	[blæʋ kol]
bump (lump)	knop	[knop]
to limp (vi)	hink	[hink]
dislocation	ontwrigting	[ontwriχtiŋ]
to dislocate (vt)	ontwrig	[ontwrəχ]

fracture	breuk	[brøək]
burn (injury)	brandwond	[brant·vont]
injury	besering	[beseriŋ]
pain, ache	pyn	[pajn]

toothache	tandpyn	[tand·pajn]
to sweat (perspire)	sweet	[sweət]
deaf (adj)	doof	[doəf]
mute (adj)	stom	[stom]

immunity	immuniteit	[immunitæjt]
virus	virus	[firus]
microbe	mikrobe	[mikrobə]
bacterium	bakterie	[bakteri]
infection	infeksie	[infeksi]

hospital	hospitaal	[hospitāl]
cure	genesing	[χenesiɳ]
to vaccinate (vt)	inent	[inɛnt]
intensive care	intensiewe sorg	[intɛnsivə sorχ]
symptom	simptoom	[simptoəm]
pulse	polsslag	[pols·slaχ]

6. Feelings. Emotions. Conversation

I, me	ek, my	[ɛk], [maj]
you	jy	[jaj]
he	hy	[haj]
she	sy	[saj]
it	dit	[dit]

we	ons	[ɔɳs]
you (to a group)	julle	[jullə]
you (polite, sing.)	u	[u]
you (polite, pl)	u	[u]
they	hulle	[hullə]

Hello! (fam.)	Hallo!	[hallo!]
Hello! (form.)	Hallo!	[hallo!]
Good morning!	Goeie môre!	[χuje mɔrə!]
Good afternoon!	Goeiemiddag!	[χuje·middaχ!]
Good evening!	Goeienaand!	[χuje·nānt!]

to say hello	dagsê	[daχsɛ:]
to greet (vt)	groet	[χrut]
How are you?	Hoe gaan dit?	[hu χãn dit?]
Goodbye!	Totsiens!	[totsiɳs!]
Bye!	Koebaai!	[kubãi!]
Thank you!	Dankie!	[danki!]

feelings	gevoelens	[χefulɛɳs]
to be hungry	honger wees	[hoɳər veəs]
to be thirsty	dors wees	[dors veəs]
tired (adj)	moeg	[muχ]
to be worried	bekommerd wees	[bekommərt veəs]

to be nervous	**senuweeagtig wees**	[senuwee·aχteχ vees]
hope	**hoop**	[hoəp]
to hope (vi, vt)	**hoop**	[hoəp]
character	**karakter**	[karaktər]
modest (adj)	**beskeie**	[beskæje]
lazy (adj)	**lui**	[lœi]
generous (adj)	**gulhartig**	[χulhartəχ]
talented (adj)	**talentvol**	[talentfol]
honest (adj)	**eerlik**	[eərlik]
serious (adj)	**ernstig**	[ɛrnstəχ]
shy, timid (adj)	**skaam**	[skām]
sincere (adj)	**opregte**	[opreχtə]
coward	**laffaard**	[laffārt]
to sleep (vi)	**slaap**	[slāp]
dream	**droom**	[droəm]
bed	**bed**	[bet]
pillow	**kussing**	[kussiŋ]
insomnia	**slaaploosheid**	[slāploəshæjt]
to go to bed	**gaan slaap**	[χān slāp]
nightmare	**nagmerrie**	[naχmerri]
alarm clock	**wekker**	[vɛkkər]
smile	**glimlag**	[χlimlaχ]
to smile (vi)	**glimlag**	[χlimlaχ]
to laugh (vi)	**lag**	[laχ]
quarrel	**rusie**	[rusi]
insult	**belediging**	[beledəχiŋ]
resentment	**gekrenktheid**	[χekrɛnkthæjt]
angry (mad)	**kwaad**	[kwāt]

7. Clothing. Personal accessories

clothes	**klere**	[klerə]
coat (overcoat)	**jas**	[jas]
fur coat	**pelsjas**	[pelʃas]
jacket (e.g., leather ~)	**baadjie**	[bādʒi]
raincoat (trenchcoat, etc.)	**reënjas**	[reɛnjas]
shirt (button shirt)	**hemp**	[hemp]
pants	**broek**	[bruk]
suit jacket	**baadjie**	[bādʒi]
suit	**pak**	[pak]
dress (frock)	**rok**	[rok]
skirt	**romp**	[romp]

T-shirt	T-hemp	[te-hemp]
bathrobe	badjas	[batjas]
pajamas	pajama	[pajama]
workwear	werksklere	[verks·klerə]

underwear	onderklere	[ondərklerə]
socks	sokkies	[sokkis]
bra	bra	[bra]
pantyhose	kousbroek	[kæʊsbruk]
stockings (thigh highs)	kouse	[kæʊsə]
bathing suit	baaikostuum	[bãj·kostɪm]
hat	hoed	[hut]
footwear	skoeisel	[skuisəl]
boots (e.g., cowboy ~)	laarse	[lãrsə]
heel	hak	[hak]
shoestring	skoenveter	[skun·fetər]
shoe polish	skoenpolitoer	[skun·politur]

cotton (n)	katoen	[katun]
wool (n)	wol	[vol]
fur (n)	bont	[bont]

gloves	handskoene	[handskunə]
mittens	duimhandskoene	[dœim·handskunə]
scarf (muffler)	serp	[serp]
glasses (eyeglasses)	bril	[bril]
umbrella	sambreel	[sambreəl]
tie (necktie)	das	[das]
handkerchief	sakdoek	[sakduk]
comb	kam	[kam]
hairbrush	haarborsel	[hãr·borsəl]

buckle	gespe	[χespə]
belt	belt	[bɛlt]
purse	beursie	[bøərsi]

collar	kraag	[krãχ]
pocket	sak	[sak]
sleeve	mou	[mæʊ]
fly (on trousers)	gulp	[χulp]

zipper (fastener)	ritssluiter	[rits·slœitər]
button	knoop	[knoəp]
to get dirty (vi)	vuil word	[fœil vort]
stain (mark, spot)	vlek	[flek]

8. City. Urban institutions

| store | winkel | [vinkəl] |
| shopping mall | winkelsentrum | [vinkəl·sentrum] |

supermarket	**supermark**	[supermark]
shoe store	**skoenwinkel**	[skun·vinkəl]
bookstore	**boekhandel**	[buk·handəl]
drugstore, pharmacy	**apteek**	[apteək]
bakery	**bakkery**	[bakkeraj]
pastry shop	**banketbakkery**	[banket·bakkeraj]
grocery store	**kruidenierswinkel**	[krœidenirs·vinkəl]
butcher shop	**slagter**	[slaχtər]
produce store	**groentewinkel**	[χruntə·vinkəl]
market	**mark**	[mark]
hair salon	**haarsalon**	[hãr·salon]
post office	**poskantoor**	[pos·kantoər]
dry cleaners	**droogskoonmakers**	[droəχ·skoən·makers]
circus	**sirkus**	[sirkus]
zoo	**dieretuin**	[dirə·tœin]
theater	**teater**	[teatər]
movie theater	**bioskoop**	[bioskoəp]
museum	**museum**	[musøəm]
library	**biblioteek**	[biblioteək]
mosque	**moskee**	[moskeə]
synagogue	**sinagoge**	[sinaχoχə]
cathedral	**katedraal**	[katedrãl]
temple	**tempel**	[tempəl]
church	**kerk**	[kerk]
college	**kollege**	[kolledʒ]
university	**universiteit**	[unifersitæjt]
school	**skool**	[skoəl]
hotel	**hotel**	[hotəl]
bank	**bank**	[bank]
embassy	**ambassade**	[ambassadə]
travel agency	**reisagentskap**	[ræjs·aχentskap]
subway	**metro**	[metro]
hospital	**hospitaal**	[hospitãl]
gas station	**petrolstasie**	[petrol·stasi]
parking lot	**parkeerterrein**	[parkeər·terræjn]
ENTRANCE	**INGANG**	[inχaŋ]
EXIT	**UITGANG**	[œitχaŋ]
PUSH	**STOOT**	[stoət]
PULL	**TREK**	[trek]
OPEN	**OOP**	[oəp]
CLOSED	**GESLUIT**	[χeslœit]
monument	**monument**	[monument]
fortress	**fort**	[fort]

palace	paleis	[palæjs]
medieval (adj)	Middeleeus	[middeliʋs]
ancient (adj)	oud	[æʋt]
national (adj)	nasionaal	[naʃionāl]
famous (monument, etc.)	bekend	[bekent]

9. Money. Finances

money	geld	[χɛlt]
coin	muntstuk	[muntstuk]
dollar	dollar	[dollar]
euro	euro	[øəro]

ATM	OTM	[o·te·em]
currency exchange	wisselkantoor	[vissəl·kantoər]
exchange rate	wisselkoers	[vissəl·kurs]
cash	kontant	[kontant]

How much?	Hoeveel?	[hufeel?]
to pay (vi, vt)	betaal	[betāl]
payment	betaling	[betaliŋ]
change (give the ~)	wisselgeld	[vissəl·χɛlt]

price	prys	[prajs]
discount	afslag	[afslaχ]
cheap (adj)	goedkoop	[χudkoəp]
expensive (adj)	duur	[dɪr]

bank	bank	[bank]
account	rekening	[rekəniŋ]
credit card	kredietkaart	[kredit·kārt]
check	tjek	[tʃek]
checkbook	tjekboek	[tʃek·buk]

debt	skuld	[skult]
debtor	skuldenaar	[skuldenār]
to lend (money)	uitleen	[œitleən]
to borrow (vi, vt)	leen	[leən]

to rent (~ a tuxedo)	verhuur	[ferhɪr]
on credit (adv)	op krediet	[op kredit]
wallet	beursie	[bøərsi]
safe	brandkas	[brant·kas]
inheritance	erfenis	[ɛrfenis]
fortune (wealth)	fortuin	[fortœin]

tax	belasting	[belastiŋ]
fine	boete	[butə]
to fine (vt)	beboet	[bebut]
wholesale (adj)	groothandels-	[χroet·handəls-]

retail (adj)	kleinhandels-	[klæjn·handəls-]
to insure (vt)	verseker	[fersekər]
insurance	versekering	[fersekeriŋ]

capital	kapitaal	[kapitãl]
turnover	omset	[omset]
stock (share)	aandeel	[ãndeəl]
profit	wins	[vins]
profitable (adj)	voordelig	[foərdeləχ]

crisis	krisis	[krisis]
bankruptcy	bankrotskap	[bankrotskap]
to go bankrupt	bankrot speel	[bankrot speəl]

accountant	boekhouer	[bukhæʊər]
salary	salaris	[salaris]
bonus (money)	bonus	[bonus]

10. Transportation

bus	bus	[bus]
streetcar	trem	[trem]
trolley bus	trembus	[trembus]

to go by ...	ry per ...	[raj pər ...]
to get on (~ the bus)	inklim	[inklim]
to get off ...	uitklim ...	[œitklim ...]

stop (e.g., bus ~)	halte	[haltə]
terminus	eindpunt	[æjnd·punt]
schedule	diensrooster	[diŋs·roəstər]
ticket	kaartjie	[kãrki]
to be late (for ...)	laat wees	[lãt veəs]

taxi, cab	taxi	[taksi]
by taxi	per taxi	[pər taksi]
taxi stand	taxistaanplek	[taksi·stãnplek]

traffic	verkeer	[ferkeər]
rush hour	spitsuur	[spits·ɪr]
to park (vi)	parkeer	[parkeər]

subway	metro	[metro]
station	stasie	[stasi]
train	trein	[træjn]
train station	treinstasie	[træjn·stasi]
rails	spoorstawe	[spoər·stavə]
compartment	kompartiment	[kompartiment]
berth	bed	[bet]
airplane	vliegtuig	[fliχtœiχ]

air ticket	lugkaartjie	[luχ·kārki]
airline	lugredery	[luχrederaj]
airport	lughawe	[luχhavə]

flight (act of flying)	vlug	[fluχ]
luggage	bagasie	[baχasi]
luggage cart	bagasiekarretjie	[baχasi·karrəki]

ship	skip	[skip]
cruise ship	toerskip	[tur·skip]
yacht	jag	[jaχ]
boat (flat-bottomed ~)	roeiboot	[ruiboət]

captain	kaptein	[kaptæjn]
cabin	kajuit	[kajœit]
port (harbor)	hawe	[havə]

bicycle	fiets	[fits]
scooter	bromponie	[bromponi]
motorcycle, bike	motorfiets	[motorfits]
pedal	pedaal	[pedāl]
pump	pomp	[pomp]
wheel	wiel	[vil]

automobile, car	motor	[motor]
ambulance	ambulans	[ambulaŋs]
truck	vragmotor	[fraχ·motor]
used (adj)	gebruik	[χebrœik]
car crash	motorbotsing	[motor·botsiŋ]
repair	herstel	[herstəl]

11. Food. Part 1

meat	vleis	[flæjs]
chicken	hoender	[hundər]
duck	eend	[eent]

pork	varkvleis	[fark·flæjs]
veal	kalfsvleis	[kalfs·flæjs]
lamb	lamsvleis	[lams·flæjs]
beef	beesvleis	[beəs·flæjs]

sausage (bologna, pepperoni, etc.)	wors	[vors]
egg	eier	[æjer]
fish	vis	[fis]
cheese	kaas	[kās]
sugar	suiker	[sœikər]
salt	sout	[sæʊt]
rice	rys	[rajs]

pasta (macaroni)	pasta	[pasta]
butter	botter	[bottər]
vegetable oil	plantaardige olie	[plantãrdiχə oli]
bread	brood	[broət]
chocolate (n)	sjokolade	[ʃokoladə]

wine	wyn	[vajn]
coffee	koffie	[koffi]
milk	melk	[melk]
juice	sap	[sap]
beer	bier	[bir]
tea	tee	[teə]

tomato	tamatie	[tamati]
cucumber	komkommer	[komkommər]
carrot	wortel	[vortəl]
potato	aartappel	[ãrtappəl]
onion	ui	[œi]
garlic	knoffel	[knoffəl]

cabbage	kool	[koəl]
beetroot	beet	[beət]
eggplant	eiervrug	[æjerfruχ]
dill	dille	[dillə]
lettuce	slaai	[slãi]
corn (maize)	mielie	[mili]

fruit	vrugte	[fruχtə]
apple	appel	[appəl]
pear	peer	[peər]
lemon	suurlemoen	[sɪr·lemun]
orange	lemoen	[lemun]
strawberry (garden ~)	aarbei	[ãrbæj]

plum	pruim	[prœim]
raspberry	framboos	[framboəs]
pineapple	pynappel	[pajnappəl]
banana	piesang	[pisaŋ]
watermelon	waatlemoen	[vãtlemun]
grape	druif	[drœif]
melon	spanspek	[spaŋspek]

12. Food. Part 2

cuisine	kookkuns	[koək·kuns]
recipe	resep	[resep]
food	kos	[kos]

| to have breakfast | ontbyt | [ontbajt] |
| to have lunch | gaan eet | [χãn eət] |

to have dinner	**aandete gebruik**	[āndetə χebrœik]
taste, flavor	**smaak**	[smāk]
tasty (adj)	**smaaklik**	[smāklik]
cold (adj)	**koud**	[kæut]
hot (adj)	**warm**	[varm]
sweet (sugary)	**soet**	[sut]
salty (adj)	**sout**	[sæut]
sandwich (bread)	**toebroodjie**	[tubroədʒi]
side dish	**sygereg**	[saj·χerəχ]
filling (for cake, pie)	**vulsel**	[fulsəl]
sauce	**sous**	[sæus]
piece (of cake, pie)	**stuk**	[stuk]
diet	**dieet**	[diət]
vitamin	**vitamien**	[fitamin]
calorie	**kalorie**	[kalori]
vegetarian (n)	**vegetariër**	[feχetariɛr]
restaurant	**restaurant**	[restɔurant]
coffee house	**koffiekroeg**	[koffi·kruχ]
appetite	**aptyt**	[aptajt]
Enjoy your meal!	**Smaaklike ete!**	[smāklikə etə!]
waiter	**kelner**	[kɛlnər]
waitress	**kelnerin**	[kɛlnərin]
bartender	**kroegman**	[kruχman]
menu	**spyskaart**	[spajs·kārt]
spoon	**lepel**	[lepəl]
knife	**mes**	[mes]
fork	**vurk**	[furk]
cup (e.g., coffee ~)	**koppie**	[koppi]
plate (dinner ~)	**bord**	[bort]
saucer	**piering**	[piriŋ]
napkin (on table)	**servet**	[serfət]
toothpick	**tandestokkie**	[tandə·stokki]
to order (meal)	**bestel**	[bestəl]
course, dish	**gereg**	[χerəχ]
portion	**porsie**	[porsi]
appetizer	**voorgereg**	[foərχerəχ]
salad	**slaai**	[slāi]
soup	**sop**	[sop]
dessert	**nagereg**	[naχerəχ]
jam (whole fruit jam)	**konfyt**	[konfajt]
ice-cream	**roomys**	[roəm·ajs]
check	**rekening**	[rekəniŋ]
to pay the check	**die rekening betaal**	[di rekeniŋ betāl]
tip	**fooitjie**	[fojki]

13. House. Apartment. Part 1

house	huis	[hœis]
country house	buitewoning	[bœitə·vonɪŋ]
villa (seaside ~)	landhuis	[land·hœis]
floor, story	verdieping	[ferdipiŋ]
entrance	ingang	[inχaŋ]
wall	muur	[mɪr]
roof	dak	[dak]
chimney	skoorsteen	[skoərsteən]
attic (storage place)	solder	[soldər]
window	venster	[fɛŋstər]
window ledge	vensterbank	[fɛŋstər·bank]
balcony	balkon	[balkon]
stairs (stairway)	trap	[trap]
mailbox	posbus	[pos·bus]
garbage can	vullisblik	[fullis·blik]
elevator	hysbak	[hajsbak]
electricity	krag, elektrisiteit	[kraχ], [elektrisitæjt]
light bulb	gloeilamp	[χlui·lamp]
switch	skakelaar	[skakəlãr]
wall socket	muurprop	[mɪrprop]
fuse	sekering	[sekəriŋ]
door	deur	[døər]
handle, doorknob	deurknop	[døər·knop]
key	sleutel	[sløətəl]
doormat	deurmat	[døər·mat]
door lock	deurslot	[døər·slot]
doorbell	deurklokkie	[døər·klokki]
knock (at the door)	klop	[klop]
to knock (vi)	klop	[klop]
peephole	loergaatjie	[lurχãki]
yard	werf	[verf]
garden	tuin	[tœin]
swimming pool	swembad	[swem·bat]
gym (home gym)	gim	[χim]
tennis court	tennisbaan	[tɛnnis·bãn]
garage	garage	[χaraʒə]
private property	privaat besit	[prifãt besit]
warning sign	waarskuwingsbord	[vãrskuviŋs·bort]
security	sekuriteit	[sekuritæjt]
security guard	veiligheidswag	[fæjliχæjts·waχ]
renovations	opknapwerk	[opknap·werk]

to renovate (vt)	opknap	[opknap]
to put in order	aan kant maak	[ān kant māk]
to paint (~ a wall)	verf	[ferf]
wallpaper	muurpapier	[mɪr·papir]
to varnish (vt)	vernis	[fernis]
pipe	pyp	[pajp]
tools	gereedskap	[χereedskap]
basement	kelder	[kɛldər]
sewerage (system)	riolering	[rioleriŋ]

14. House. Apartment. Part 2

apartment	woonstel	[voəŋstəl]
room	kamer	[kamər]
bedroom	slaapkamer	[slāp·kamər]
dining room	eetkamer	[eet·kamər]
living room	sitkamer	[sit·kamər]
study (home office)	studeerkamer	[studeər·kamər]
entry room	ingangsportaal	[inχaŋs·portāl]
bathroom (room with a bath or shower)	badkamer	[bad·kamər]
half bath	toilet	[tojlet]
floor	vloer	[flur]
ceiling	plafon	[plafon]
to dust (vt)	afstof	[afstof]
vacuum cleaner	stofsuier	[stof·sœiər]
to vacuum (vt)	stofsuig	[stofsœiχ]
mop	mop	[mop]
dust cloth	stoflap	[stoflap]
short broom	kort besem	[kort besem]
dustpan	skoppie	[skoppi]
furniture	meubels	[møəbɛls]
table	tafel	[tafel]
chair	stoel	[stul]
armchair	gemakstoel	[χemak·stul]
bookcase	boekkas	[buk·kas]
shelf	rak	[rak]
wardrobe	klerekas	[klerə·kas]
mirror	spieël	[spiɛl]
carpet	mat	[mat]
fireplace	vuurherd	[fɪr·hert]
drapes	gordyne	[χordajnə]

| table lamp | tafellamp | [tafel·lamp] |
| chandelier | kroonlugter | [kroən·luχtər] |

kitchen	kombuis	[kombœis]
gas stove (range)	gasstoof	[χɑs·stoəf]
electric stove	elektriese stoof	[elektrisə stoəf]
microwave oven	mikrogolfoond	[mikroχolf·oent]

refrigerator	yskas	[ajs·kas]
freezer	vrieskas	[friskas]
dishwasher	skottelgoedwasser	[skottɛlχud·wassər]
faucet	kraan	[krān]

meat grinder	vleismeul	[flæjs·møəl]
juicer	versapper	[fersappər]
toaster	broodrooster	[broəd·roəstər]
mixer	menger	[meŋər]

coffee machine	koffiemasjien	[koffi·maʃin]
kettle	fluitketel	[flœit·ketəl]
teapot	teepot	[teə·pot]

TV set	TV-stel	[te·fe·stəl]
VCR (video recorder)	videomasjien	[video·maʃin]
iron (e.g., steam ~)	strykyster	[strajk·ajstər]
telephone	telefoon	[telefoən]

15. Professions. Social status

director	direkteur	[direktøər]
superior	hoof	[hoəf]
president	direkteur	[direktøər]
assistant	assistent	[assistent]
secretary	sekretaris	[sekretaris]

owner, proprietor	eienaar	[æjenār]
partner	vennoot	[fɛnnoət]
stockholder	aandeelhouer	[āndeəl·hæʊər]

businessman	sakeman	[sakəman]
millionaire	miljoenêr	[miljunær]
billionaire	miljardêr	[miljardær]

actor	akteur	[aktøər]
architect	argitek	[arχitek]
banker	bankier	[bankir]
broker	makelaar	[makəlār]

| veterinarian | veearts | [feə·arts] |
| doctor | dokter | [doktər] |

chambermaid	kamermeisie	[kamər·mæjsi]
designer	ontwerper	[ontwerpər]
correspondent	korrespondent	[korrespondɛnt]
delivery man	koerier	[kurir]

electrician	elektrisiën	[ɛlektrisiɛn]
musician	musikant	[musikant]
babysitter	babasitter	[babasittər]
hairdresser	haarkapper	[hār·kappər]
herder, shepherd	herder	[herdər]

singer (masc.)	sanger	[saŋər]
translator	vertaler	[fertalər]
writer	skrywer	[skrajvər]
carpenter	timmerman	[timmerman]
cook	kok	[kok]

fireman	brandweerman	[brantveer·man]
police officer	polisieman	[polisi·man]
mailman	posbode	[pos·bodə]
programmer	programmeur	[proχrammøər]
salesman (store staff)	verkoper	[ferkopər]

worker	werker	[verkər]
gardener	tuinman	[tœin·man]
plumber	loodgieter	[loedχitər]
dentist	tandarts	[tand·arts]
flight attendant (fem.)	lugwaardin	[luχ·wārdin]

dancer (masc.)	danser	[daŋsər]
bodyguard	lyfwag	[lajf·waχ]
scientist	wetenskaplike	[vetɛŋskaplikə]
schoolteacher	onderwyser	[ondərwajsər]

farmer	boer	[bur]
surgeon	chirurg	[ʃirurχ]
miner	mynwerker	[majn·werkər]
chef (kitchen chef)	sjef	[ʃef]
driver	bestuurder	[bestɪrdər]

16. Sport

kind of sports	sportsoorte	[sport·soərtə]
soccer	sokker	[sokkər]
hockey	hokkie	[hokki]
basketball	basketbal	[basketbal]
baseball	bofbal	[bofbal]

volleyball	vlugbal	[fluχbal]
boxing	boks	[boks]

wrestling	stoei	[stui]
tennis	tennis	[tɛnnis]
swimming	swem	[swem]

chess	skaak	[skãk]
running	hardloop	[hardloəp]
athletics	atletiek	[atletik]
figure skating	kunsskaats	[kuns·skãts]
cycling	fiets	[fits]

billiards	biljart	[biljart]
bodybuilding	liggaamsbou	[liχχãmsbæʊ]
golf	gholf	[golf]
scuba diving	duik	[dœik]
sailing	seil	[sæjl]
archery	boogskiet	[boəχ·skit]

period, half	helfte	[hɛlftə]
half-time	rustyd	[rustajt]
tie	gelykspel	[χelajkspəl]
to tie (vi)	gelykop speel	[χelajkop speəl]

treadmill	trapmeul	[trapmøəl]
player	speler	[spelər]
substitute	plaasvervanger	[plãs·ferfaŋər]
substitutes bench	plaasvervangersbank	[plãs·ferfaŋərs·bank]

match	wedstryd	[vedstrajt]
goal	doel	[dul]
goalkeeper	doelwagter	[dul·waχtər]
goal (score)	doelpunt	[dulpunt]

| Olympic Games | Olimpiese Spele | [olimpisə spelə] |
| final | finale | [finalə] |

| champion | kampioen | [kampiun] |
| championship | kampioenskap | [kampiunskap] |

winner	oorwinnaar	[oərwinnãr]
victory	oorwinning	[oərwinniŋ]
to win (vi)	wen	[ven]
to lose (not win)	verloor	[ferloər]
medal	medalje	[medalje]
first place	eerste plek	[eərstə plek]

| second place | tweede plek | [tweədə plek] |
| third place | derde plek | [derdə plek] |

stadium	stadion	[stadion]
fan, supporter	ondersteuner	[ondərstøənər]
trainer, coach	breier	[bræjer]
training	oefen	[ufən]

17. Foreign languages. Orthography

language	**taal**	[tãl]
to study (vt)	**studeer**	[studeər]
pronunciation	**uitspraak**	[œitsprãk]
accent	**aksent**	[aksent]
noun	**selfstandige naamwoord**	[sɛlfstandiχə nãmwoərt]
adjective	**byvoeglike naamwoord**	[bajfuχlikə nãmvoərt]
verb	**werkwoord**	[verk·woərt]
adverb	**bijwoord**	[bij·woərt]
pronoun	**voornaamwoord**	[foərnãm·voərt]
interjection	**tussenwerpsel**	[tussən·werpsəl]
preposition	**voorsetsel**	[foərsetsəl]
root	**stam**	[stam]
ending	**agtervoegsel**	[aχtər·fuχsəl]
prefix	**voorvoegsel**	[foər·fuχsəl]
syllable	**lettergreep**	[lɛttər·χreəp]
suffix	**agtervoegsel, suffiks**	[aχtər·fuχsəl], [suffiks]
stress mark	**klemteken**	[klem·tekən]
period, dot	**punt**	[punt]
comma	**komma**	[komma]
colon	**dubbelpunt**	[dubbəl·punt]
ellipsis	**beletselteken**	[beletsəl·tekən]
question	**vraag**	[frãχ]
question mark	**vraagteken**	[frãχ·tekən]
exclamation point	**uitroepteken**	[œitrup·tekən]
in quotation marks	**tussen aanhalingstekens**	[tussən ãnhaliŋs·tekəŋs]
in parenthesis	**tussen hakies**	[tussən hakis]
letter	**letter**	[lɛttər]
capital letter	**hoofletter**	[hoəf·lɛttər]
sentence	**sin**	[sin]
group of words	**woordgroep**	[voərt·χrup]
expression	**uitdrukking**	[œitdrukkiŋ]
subject	**onderwerp**	[ondərwerp]
predicate	**predikaat**	[predikãt]
line	**reël**	[reɛl]
paragraph	**paragraaf**	[paraχrãf]
synonym	**sinoniem**	[sinonim]
antonym	**antoniem**	[antonim]
exception	**uitsondering**	[œitsondəriŋ]
to underline (vt)	**onderstreep**	[ondərstreəp]
rules	**reëls**	[reɛls]

grammar	grammatika	[χrammatika]
vocabulary	woordeskat	[voərdeskat]
phonetics	fonetika	[fonetika]
alphabet	alfabet	[alfabet]
textbook	handboek	[hɑnd·buk]
dictionary	woordeboek	[voərdə·buk]
phrasebook	taalgids	[tāl·χids]

word	woord	[voərt]
meaning	betekenis	[betekənis]
memory	geheue	[χəhøə]

18. The Earth. Geography

the Earth	die Aarde	[di ãrdə]
the globe (the Earth)	die aardbol	[di ãrdbol]
planet	planeet	[planeət]

geography	geografie	[χeoχrafi]
nature	natuur	[natr]
map	kaart	[kãrt]
atlas	atlas	[atlas]

in the north	in die noorde	[in di noərdə]
in the south	in die suide	[in di sœidə]
in the west	in die weste	[in di vestə]
in the east	in die ooste	[in di oəstə]

sea	see	[seə]
ocean	oseaan	[oseãn]
gulf (bay)	golf	[χolf]
straits	straat	[strãt]

continent (mainland)	kontinent	[kontinent]
island	eiland	[æjlant]
peninsula	skiereiland	[skir·æjlant]
archipelago	argipel	[arχipəl]

harbor	hawe	[havə]
coral reef	koraalrif	[korãl·rif]
shore	oewer	[uvər]
coast	kus	[kus]

| flow (flood tide) | hoogwater | [hoəχ·vatər] |
| ebb (ebb tide) | laagwater | [lãχ·vatər] |

latitude	breedtegraad	[breədtə·χrãt]
longitude	lengtegraad	[leɳtə·χrãt]
parallel	parallel	[paralləl]
equator	ewenaar	[ɛvenãr]

sky	hemel	[heməl]
horizon	horison	[horison]
atmosphere	atmosfeer	[atmosfeər]
mountain	berg	[berχ]
summit, top	top	[top]
cliff	krans	[kraŋs]
hill	kop	[kop]
volcano	vulkaan	[fulkān]
glacier	gletser	[χletsər]
waterfall	waterval	[vatər·fal]
plain	vlakte	[flaktə]
river	rivier	[rifir]
spring (natural source)	bron	[bron]
bank (of river)	oewer	[uvər]
downstream (adv)	stroomafwaarts	[stroəm·afvārts]
upstream (adv)	stroomopwaarts	[stroəm·opvārts]
lake	meer	[meər]
dam	damwal	[dam·wal]
canal	kanaal	[kanāl]
swamp (marshland)	moeras	[muras]
ice	ys	[ajs]

19. Countries of the world. Part 1

Europe	Europa	[øəropa]
European Union	Europese Unie	[øəropesə uni]
European (n)	Europeaan	[øəropeān]
European (adj)	Europees	[øəropeəs]
Austria	Oostenryk	[oestenrajk]
Great Britain	Groot-Brittanje	[χroət-brittanje]
England	Engeland	[ɛŋəlant]
Belgium	België	[belχiɛ]
Germany	Duitsland	[dœitslant]
Netherlands	Nederland	[nedərlant]
Holland	Holland	[hollant]
Greece	Griekeland	[χrikəlant]
Denmark	Denemarke	[denemarkə]
Ireland	Ierland	[irlant]
Iceland	Ysland	[ajslant]
Spain	Spanje	[spanje]
Italy	Italië	[italiɛ]
Cyprus	Ciprus	[siprus]
Malta	Malta	[malta]

Norway	Noorweë	[noərwɛ]
Portugal	Portugal	[portuχal]
Finland	Finland	[finlant]
France	Frankryk	[frankrajk]
Sweden	Swede	[swedə]

Switzerland	Switserland	[switsərlant]
Scotland	Skotland	[skotlant]
Vatican	Vatikaan	[fatikān]
Liechtenstein	Lichtenstein	[liχtɛŋstejn]
Luxembourg	Luksemburg	[luksemburχ]

Monaco	Monako	[monako]
Albania	Albanië	[albaniɛ]
Bulgaria	Bulgarye	[bulχaraje]
Hungary	Hongarye	[honχaraje]
Latvia	Letland	[letlant]

Lithuania	Litoue	[litæʊə]
Poland	Pole	[polə]
Romania	Roemenië	[rumeniɛ]
Serbia	Serwië	[serwiɛ]
Slovakia	Slowakye	[slovakaje]

Croatia	Kroasië	[kroasiɛ]
Czech Republic	Tjeggië	[ʧeχiɛ]
Estonia	Estland	[ɛstlant]
Bosnia and Herzegovina	Bosnië & Herzegowina	[bosniɛ en hersegovina]
Macedonia (Republic of ~)	Masedonië	[masedoniɛ]

Slovenia	Slovenië	[slofeniɛ]
Montenegro	Montenegro	[montənegro]
Belarus	Belarus	[belarus]
Moldova, Moldavia	Moldawië	[moldaviɛ]
Russia	Rusland	[ruslant]
Ukraine	Oekraïne	[ukraïnə]

20. Countries of the world. Part 2

Asia	Asië	[asiɛ]
Vietnam	Viëtnam	[viɛtnam]
India	Indië	[indiɛ]
Israel	Israel	[israəl]
China	Sjina	[ʃina]

Lebanon	Libanon	[libanon]
Mongolia	Mongolië	[monχoliɛ]
Malaysia	Maleisië	[malæjsiɛ]
Pakistan	Pakistan	[pakistan]
Saudi Arabia	Saoedi-Arabië	[saudi-arabiɛ]

Thailand	Thailand	[tajlant]
Taiwan	Taiwan	[tajvan]
Turkey	Turkye	[turkaje]
Japan	Japan	[japan]
Afghanistan	Afghanistan	[afχanistan]
Bangladesh	Bangladesj	[bangladeʃ]
Indonesia	Indonesië	[indonesiɛ]
Jordan	Jordanië	[jordaniɛ]
Iraq	Irak	[irak]
Iran	Iran	[iran]
Cambodia	Kambodja	[kambodja]
Kuwait	Kuwait	[kuvajt]
Laos	Laos	[laos]
Myanmar	Myanmar	[mjanmar]
Nepal	Nepal	[nepal]
United Arab Emirates	Verenigde Arabiese Emirate	[fereniχde arabise emirate]
Syria	Sirië	[siriɛ]
Palestine	Palestina	[palestina]
South Korea	Suid-Korea	[sœid-korea]
North Korea	Noord-Korea	[noerd-korea]
United States of America	Verenigde State van Amerika	[fereniχde state fan amerika]
Canada	Kanada	[kanada]
Mexico	Meksiko	[meksiko]
Argentina	Argentinië	[arχentiniɛ]
Brazil	Brasilië	[brasiliɛ]
Colombia	Colombia, Kolombië	[kolombia], [kolombiɛ]
Cuba	Kuba	[kuba]
Chile	Chili	[tʃili]
Venezuela	Venezuela	[fenesuela]
Ecuador	Ecuador	[ɛkuador]
The Bahamas	die Bahamas	[di bahamas]
Panama	Panama	[panama]
Egypt	Egipte	[ɛχipte]
Morocco	Marokko	[marokko]
Tunisia	Tunisië	[tunisiɛ]
Kenya	Kenia	[kenia]
Libya	Libië	[libiɛ]
South Africa	Suid-Afrika	[sœid-afrika]
Australia	Australië	[ɔustraliɛ]
New Zealand	Nieu-Seeland	[niu-seelant]

21. Weather. Natural disasters

weather	weer	[veər]
weather forecast	weersvoorspelling	[veərs·foərspɛlliŋ]
temperature	temperatuur	[təmperatɪr]
thermometer	termometer	[termometər]
barometer	barometer	[barometər]

sun	son	[son]
to shine (vi)	skyn	[skajn]
sunny (day)	sonnig	[sonnəχ]
to come up (vi)	opkom	[opkom]
to set (vi)	ondergaan	[ondərχãn]

rain	reën	[rɛɛn]
it's raining	dit reën	[dit rɛɛn]
pouring rain	stortbui	[stortbœi]
rain cloud	reënwolk	[rɛɛn·wolk]
puddle	poeletjie	[puləki]
to get wet (in rain)	nat word	[nat vort]

thunderstorm	donderstorm	[dondər·storm]
lightning (~ strike)	weerlig	[veərləχ]
to flash (vi)	flits	[flits]
thunder	donder	[dondər]
it's thundering	dit donder	[dit dondər]
hail	hael	[haəl]
it's hailing	dit hael	[dit haəl]

heat (extreme ~)	hitte	[hittə]
it's hot	dis vrekwarm	[dis frekvarm]
it's warm	dit is warm	[dit is varm]
it's cold	dis koud	[dis kæʊt]

fog (mist)	mis	[mis]
foggy	mistig	[mistəχ]
cloud	wolk	[volk]
cloudy (adj)	bewolk	[bevolk]
humidity	vogtigheid	[foχtiχæjt]

snow	sneeu	[sniʊ]
it's snowing	dit sneeu	[dit sniʊ]
frost (severe ~, freezing cold)	ryp	[rajp]
below zero (adv)	onder nul	[ondər nul]
hoarfrost	ruigryp	[rœiχ·rajp]

bad weather	slegte weer	[sleχtə veər]
disaster	ramp	[ramp]
flood, inundation	oorstroming	[oərstromiŋ]
avalanche	lawine	[lavinə]

earthquake	aardbewing	[ārd·beviŋ]
tremor, quake	aardskok	[ārd·skok]
epicenter	episentrum	[ɛpisentrum]
eruption	uitbarsting	[œitbarstiŋ]
lava	lawa	[lava]

twister, tornado	tornado	[tornado]
hurricane	orkaan	[orkān]
tsunami	tsunami	[tsunami]
cyclone	sikloon	[sikloən]

22. Animals. Part 1

| animal | dier | [dir] |
| predator | roofdier | [roəf·dir] |

tiger	tier	[tir]
lion	leeu	[liʊ]
wolf	wolf	[volf]
fox	vos	[fos]
jaguar	jaguar	[jaχuar]

lynx	los	[los]
coyote	prêriewolf	[præri·volf]
jackal	jakkals	[jakkals]
hyena	hiëna	[hiɛna]

squirrel	eekhoring	[eəkhoriŋ]
hedgehog	krimpvarkie	[krimpfarki]
rabbit	konyn	[konajn]
raccoon	wasbeer	[vasbeər]

hamster	hamster	[hamstər]
mole	mol	[mol]
mouse	muis	[mœis]
rat	rot	[rot]
bat	vlermuis	[fler·mœis]

beaver	bewer	[bevər]
horse	perd	[pert]
deer	hert	[hert]
camel	kameel	[kameəl]
zebra	sebra, kwagga	[sebra], [kwaχχa]

whale	walvis	[valfis]
seal	seehond	[seə·hont]
walrus	walrus	[valrus]
dolphin	dolfyn	[dolfajn]
bear	beer	[beər]
monkey	aap	[āp]

elephant	olifant	[olifant]
rhinoceros	renoster	[renostər]
giraffe	kameelperd	[kameəl·pert]

hippopotamus	seekoei	[see·kui]
kangaroo	kangaroe	[kaŋχaru]
cat	kat	[kat]
dog	hond	[hont]

cow	koei	[kui]
bull	bul	[bul]
sheep (ewe)	skaap	[skãp]
goat	bok	[bok]

donkey	donkie, esel	[donki], [eisəl]
pig, hog	vark	[fark]
hen (chicken)	hoender, hen	[hundər], [hen]
rooster	haan	[hãn]

duck	eend	[eent]
goose	gans	[χaŋs]
turkey (hen)	kalkoen	[kalkun]
sheepdog	herdershond	[herdərs·hont]

23. Animals. Part 2

bird	voël	[foɛl]
pigeon	duif	[dœif]
sparrow	mossie	[mossi]
tit (great tit)	mees	[meəs]
magpie	ekster	[ɛkstər]

eagle	arend	[arɛnt]
hawk	sperwer	[sperwər]
falcon	valk	[falk]

swan	swaan	[swãn]
crane	kraanvoël	[krãn·foɛl]
stork	ooievaar	[ojefãr]
parrot	papegaai	[papəχãi]
peacock	pou	[pæʋ]
ostrich	volstruis	[folstrœis]

heron	reier	[ræjer]
nightingale	nagtegaal	[naχteχãl]
swallow	swael	[swaəl]
woodpecker	speg	[speχ]
cuckoo	koekoek	[kukuk]
owl	uil	[œil]
penguin	pikkewyn	[pikkəvajn]

tuna	**tuna**	[tuna]
trout	**forel**	[forəl]
eel	**paling**	[paliŋ]

shark	**haai**	[hãi]
crab	**krap**	[krap]
jellyfish	**jellievis**	[jelli·fis]
octopus	**seekat**	[see·kat]

starfish	**seester**	[see·stər]
sea urchin	**see-egel, seekastaiing**	[see-eɣel], [see·kastajiŋ]
seahorse	**seeperdjie**	[see·perdʒi]
shrimp	**garnaal**	[ɣarnãl]

snake	**slang**	[slaŋ]
viper	**adder**	[addər]
lizard	**akkedis**	[akkedis]
iguana	**leguaan**	[leɣuãn]
chameleon	**verkleurmannetjie**	[ferkløər·manneki]
scorpion	**skerpioen**	[skerpiun]

turtle	**skilpad**	[skilpat]
frog	**padda**	[padda]
crocodile	**krokodil**	[krokodil]

insect, bug	**insek**	[insek]
butterfly	**skoenlapper**	[skunlappər]
ant	**mier**	[mir]
fly	**vlieg**	[fliɣ]

mosquito	**muskiet**	[muskit]
beetle	**kewer**	[kevər]
bee	**by**	[baj]
spider	**spinnekop**	[spinnə·kop]

24. Trees. Plants

tree	**boom**	[boəm]
birch	**berk**	[berk]
oak	**eik**	[æjk]
linden tree	**lindeboom**	[lində·boəm]
aspen	**trilpopulier**	[trilpopulir]

maple	**esdoring**	[ɛsdoriŋ]
spruce	**spar**	[spar]
pine	**denneboom**	[dɛnnə·boəm]
cedar	**seder**	[sedər]

poplar	**populier**	[populir]
rowan	**lysterbessie**	[lajstərbɛssi]

beech	**beuk**	[bøək]
elm	**olm**	[olm]
ash (tree)	**esboom**	[ɛs·boəm]
chestnut	**kastaiing**	[kastajiŋ]
palm tree	**palm**	[pɑlm]
bush	**struik**	[strœik]
mushroom	**paddastoel**	[paddastul]
poisonous mushroom	**giftige paddastoel**	[χiftiχə paddastul]
cep (Boletus edulis)	**Eetbare boleet**	[eetbarə boleət]
russula	**russula**	[russula]
fly agaric	**vlieëswam**	[fliɛ·swam]
death cap	**duiwelsbrood**	[dœivɛls·broət]
flower	**blom**	[blom]
bouquet (of flowers)	**boeket**	[buket]
rose (flower)	**roos**	[roəs]
tulip	**tulp**	[tulp]
carnation	**angelier**	[anχəlir]
camomile	**kamille**	[kamillə]
cactus	**kaktus**	[kaktus]
lily of the valley	**dallelie**	[dalleli]
snowdrop	**sneeuklokkie**	[sniʊ·klokki]
water lily	**waterlelie**	[vatər·leli]
greenhouse (tropical ~)	**broeikas**	[bruikas]
lawn	**grasperk**	[χras·perk]
flowerbed	**blombed**	[blom·bet]
plant	**plant**	[plant]
grass	**gras**	[χras]
leaf	**blaar**	[blãr]
petal	**kroonblaar**	[kroən·blãr]
stem	**stingel**	[stiŋəl]
young plant (shoot)	**saailing**	[sãjliŋ]
cereal crops	**graangewasse**	[χrãn·χəwassə]
wheat	**koring**	[koriŋ]
rye	**rog**	[roχ]
oats	**hawer**	[havər]
millet	**gierst**	[χirst]
barley	**gars**	[χars]
corn	**mielie**	[mili]
rice	**rys**	[rajs]

25. Various useful words

balance (of situation)	**balans**	[balaŋs]
base (basis)	**basis**	[basis]

beginning	**begin**	[beχin]
category	**kategorie**	[kateχori]

choice	**keuse**	[køəsə]
coincidence	**toeval**	[tufal]
comparison	**vergelyking**	[ferχelajkiŋ]
degree (extent, amount)	**graad**	[χrãt]

development	**ontwikkeling**	[ontwikkeliŋ]
difference	**verskil**	[ferskil]
effect (e.g., of drugs)	**effek**	[ɛffek]
effort (exertion)	**inspanning**	[inspanniŋ]

element	**element**	[ɛlement]
example (illustration)	**voorbeeld**	[foərbeəlt]
fact	**feit**	[fæjt]
help	**hulp**	[hulp]

ideal	**ideaal**	[ideãl]
kind (sort, type)	**soort**	[soərt]
mistake, error	**fout**	[fæʊt]
moment	**moment**	[moment]

obstacle	**hinderpaal**	[hindərpãl]
part (~ of sth)	**deel**	[deəl]
pause (break)	**pouse**	[pæʊsə]
position	**posisie**	[posisi]

problem	**probleem**	[probleəm]
process	**proses**	[proses]
progress	**vooruitgang**	[foərœitχaŋ]
property (quality)	**eienskap**	[æjeŋskap]

reaction	**reaksie**	[reaksi]
risk	**risiko**	[risiko]
secret	**geheim**	[χəhæjm]
series	**reeks**	[reəks]

shape (outer form)	**vorm**	[form]
situation	**toestand**	[tustant]
solution	**oplossing**	[oplossiŋ]
standard (adj)	**standaard**	[standãrt]

stop (pause)	**pouse**	[pæʊsə]
style	**styl**	[stajl]
system	**sisteem**	[sisteəm]
table (chart)	**tabel**	[tabəl]
tempo, rate	**tempo**	[tempo]

term (word, expression)	**term**	[term]
truth (e.g., moment of ~)	**waarheid**	[vãrhæjt]

turn (please wait your ~)	beurt	[bøərt]
urgent (adj)	dringend	[driŋən]

utility (usefulness)	nut	[nut]
variant (alternative)	variant	[fariant]
way (means, method)	manier	[manir]
zone	sone	[sonə]

26. Modifiers. Adjectives. Part 1

additional (adj)	addisioneel	[addiʃioneəl]
ancient (~ civilization)	antiek	[antik]
artificial (adj)	kunsmatig	[kunsmatəχ]
bad (adj)	sleg	[sleχ]
beautiful (person)	pragtig	[praχtəχ]

big (in size)	groot	[χroət]
bitter (taste)	bitter	[bittər]
blind (sightless)	blind	[blint]
central (adj)	sentraal	[sentrāl]

children's (adj)	kinder-	[kindər-]
clandestine (secret)	agterbaks	[aχtərbaks]
clean (free from dirt)	skoon	[skoən]
clever (smart)	slim	[slim]
compatible (adj)	verenigbaar	[ferenixbār]

contented (satisfied)	tevrede	[tefredə]
dangerous (adj)	gevaarlik	[χefārlik]
dead (not alive)	dood	[doət]
dense (fog, smoke)	dig	[diχ]
difficult (decision)	moeilik	[muilik]

dirty (not clean)	vuil	[fœil]
easy (not difficult)	maklik	[maklik]
empty (glass, room)	leeg	[leəχ]
exact (amount)	juis	[jœis]
excellent (adj)	uitstekend	[œitstekent]

excessive (adj)	oormatig	[oərmatəχ]
exterior (adj)	buite-	[bœite-]
fast (quick)	vinnig	[finnəχ]
fertile (land, soil)	vrugbaar	[fruχbār]
fragile (china, glass)	breekbaar	[breəkbār]

free (at no cost)	gratis	[χratis]
fresh (~ water)	vars	[fars]
frozen (food)	gevries	[χefris]
full (completely filled)	vol	[fol]
happy (adj)	gelukkig	[χelukkəχ]

hard (not soft)	hard	[hart]
huge (adj)	kolossaal	[kolossāl]
ill (sick, unwell)	siek	[sik]
immobile (adj)	doodstil	[doədstil]
important (adj)	belangrik	[belaŋrik]

interior (adj)	binne-	[binne-]
last (e.g., ~ week)	laas-	[lās-]
last (final)	laaste	[lāstə]
left (e.g., ~ side)	linker-	[linkər-]
legal (legitimate)	wetlik	[vetlik]

light (in weight)	lig	[liχ]
liquid (fluid)	vloeibaar	[fluibār]
long (e.g., ~ hair)	lang	[laŋ]
loud (voice, etc.)	hard	[hart]
low (voice)	sag	[saχ]

27. Modifiers. Adjectives. Part 2

main (principal)	hoof-	[hoəf-]
matt, matte	mat	[mat]
mysterious (adj)	raaiselagtig	[rājselaχtəχ]
narrow (street, etc.)	smal	[smal]
native (~ country)	geboorte-	[χeboərtə-]

negative (~ response)	negatief	[neχatif]
new (adj)	nuut	[nɪt]
next (e.g., ~ week)	volgend	[folχent]
normal (adj)	normaal	[normāl]
not difficult (adj)	nie moeilik nie	[ni muilik ni]

obligatory (adj)	verplig	[ferpləχ]
old (house)	ou	[æʊ]
open (adj)	oop	[oəp]
opposite (adj)	teenoorgestel	[teənoərχestəl]
ordinary (usual)	gewoon	[χevoən]

original (unusual)	oorspronklik	[oərspronklik]
personal (adj)	persoonlik	[persoənlik]
polite (adj)	beleefd	[beleəft]
poor (not rich)	arm	[arm]

possible (adj)	moontlik	[moentlik]
principal (main)	vernaamste	[fernāmstə]
probable (adj)	waarskynlik	[vārskajnlik]
prolonged (e.g., ~ applause)	langdurig	[laŋdurəχ]
public (open to all)	openbaar	[openbār]
rare (adj)	seldsaam	[sɛldsām]

raw (uncooked)	rou	[ræʊ]
right (not left)	regter	[reχtər]
ripe (fruit)	ryp	[rajp]

risky (adj)	riskant	[riskant]
sad (~ look)	droewig	[druvəχ]
second hand (adj)	gebruik	[χebrœik]
shallow (water)	vlak	[flak]
sharp (blade, etc.)	skerp	[skerp]

short (in length)	kort	[kort]
similar (adj)	eenders	[eənders]
small (in size)	klein	[klæjn]
smooth (surface)	glad	[χlat]
soft (~ toys)	sag	[saχ]

solid (~ wall)	stewig	[stevəχ]
sour (flavor, taste)	suur	[sɪr]
spacious (house, etc.)	ruim	[rœim]
special (adj)	spesiaal	[spesiāl]

straight (line, road)	reg	[reχ]
strong (person)	sterk	[sterk]
stupid (foolish)	dom	[dom]
superb, perfect (adj)	uitstekend	[œitstekent]

sweet (sugary)	soet	[sut]
tan (adj)	bruingebrand	[brœiŋəbrant]
tasty (delicious)	smaaklik	[smāklik]
unclear (adj)	onduidelik	[ondœidelik]

28. Verbs. Part 1

to accuse (vt)	beskuldig	[beskuldəχ]
to agree (say yes)	saamstem	[sāmstem]
to announce (vt)	aankondig	[ānkondəχ]
to answer (vi, vt)	antwoord	[antwoert]
to apologize (vi)	verskoning vra	[ferskoniŋ fra]

to arrive (vi)	aankom	[ānkom]
to ask (~ oneself)	vra	[fra]
to be absent	afwesig wees	[afwesəχ veəs]
to be afraid	bang wees	[baŋ veəs]
to be born	gebore word	[χebore vort]

to be in a hurry	haastig wees	[hāstəχ veəs]
to beat (to hit)	slaan	[slān]
to begin (vt)	begin	[beχin]
to believe (in God)	glo	[χlo]
to belong to ...	behoort aan ...	[behoert ān ...]

to break (split into pieces)	**breek**	[breək]
to build (vt)	**bou**	[bæʋ]
to buy (purchase)	**koop**	[koəp]
can (v aux)	**kan**	[kan]
can (v aux)	**kan**	[kan]
to cancel (call off)	**kanselleer**	[kaŋsɛlleər]
to catch (vt)	**vang**	[faŋ]
to change (vt)	**verander**	[ferandər]
to check (to examine)	**nagaan**	[naχān]
to choose (select)	**kies**	[kis]
to clean up (tidy)	**skoonmaak**	[skoənmāk]
to close (vt)	**sluit**	[slœit]
to compare (vt)	**vergelyk**	[ferχəlajk]
to complain (vi, vt)	**kla**	[kla]
to confirm (vt)	**bevestig**	[befestəχ]
to congratulate (vt)	**gelukwens**	[χelukwɛŋs]
to cook (dinner)	**kook**	[koək]
to copy (vt)	**kopieer**	[kopir]
to cost (vt)	**kos**	[kos]
to count (add up)	**tel**	[təl]
to count on …	**reken op …**	[reken op …]
to create (vt)	**skep**	[skep]
to cry (weep)	**huil**	[hœil]
to dance (vi, vt)	**dans**	[daŋs]
to deceive (vi, vt)	**bedrieg**	[bedrəχ]
to decide (~ to do sth)	**beslis**	[beslis]
to delete (vt)	**uitvee**	[œitfeə]
to demand (request firmly)	**eis**	[æjs]
to deny (vt)	**ontken**	[ontken]
to depend on …	**afhang van …**	[afhaŋ fan …]
to despise (vt)	**minag**	[minaχ]
to die (vi)	**doodgaan**	[doədχān]
to dig (vt)	**grawe**	[χravə]
to disappear (vi)	**verdwyn**	[ferdwajn]
to discuss (vt)	**bespreek**	[bespreək]
to disturb (vt)	**steur**	[støər]

29. Verbs. Part 2

to dive (vi)	**duik**	[dœik]
to divorce (vi)	**skei**	[skæj]
to do (vt)	**doen**	[dun]
to doubt (have doubts)	**twyfel**	[twajfəl]
to drink (vi, vt)	**drink**	[drink]

to drop (let fall)	laat val	[lāt fal]
to dry (clothes, hair)	droog	[droəχ]
to eat (vi, vt)	eet	[eət]
to end (~ a relationship)	beëindig	[beɛindəχ]
to excuse (forgive)	verskoon	[ferskoən]

to exist (vi)	bestaan	[bɘstān]
to expect (foresee)	voorsien	[foərsin]
to explain (vt)	verduidelik	[ferdœeidəlik]
to fall (vi)	val	[fal]
to fight (street fight, etc.)	baklei	[baklæj]
to find (vt)	vind	[fint]

to finish (vt)	klaarmaak	[klārmāk]
to fly (vi)	vlieg	[fliχ]
to forbid (vt)	verbied	[ferbit]
to forget (vi, vt)	vergeet	[ferχeət]
to forgive (vt)	vergewe	[ferχevə]

to get tired	moeg word	[muχ vort]
to give (vt)	gee	[χeə]
to go (on foot)	gaan	[χān]
to hate (vt)	haat	[hāt]

to have (vt)	hê	[hɛ:]
to have breakfast	ontbyt	[ontbajt]
to have dinner	aandete gebruik	[āndetə χebrœik]
to have lunch	gaan eet	[χān eət]

to hear (vt)	hoor	[hoər]
to help (vt)	help	[hɛlp]
to hide (vt)	wegsteek	[veχsteək]
to hope (vi, vt)	hoop	[hoəp]
to hunt (vi, vt)	jag	[jaχ]
to hurry (vi)	opskud	[opskut]

to insist (vi, vt)	aandring	[āndriŋ]
to insult (vt)	beledig	[beledəχ]
to invite (vt)	uitnooi	[œitnoj]
to joke (vi)	grappies maak	[χrappis māk]
to keep (vt)	bewaar	[bevār]

to kill (vt)	doodmaak	[doədmāk]
to know (sb)	ken	[ken]
to know (sth)	weet	[veət]
to like (I like …)	hou van	[hæʊ fan]
to look at …	kyk na …	[kajk na …]

to lose (umbrella, etc.)	verloor	[ferloər]
to love (sb)	liefhê	[lifhɛ:]
to meet (vi, vt)	ontmoet	[ontmut]
to miss (school, etc.)	bank	[bank]

30. Verbs. Part 3

to obey (vi, vt)	gehoorsaam	[χehoərsãm]
to open (vt)	oopmaak	[oəpmãk]
to participate (vi)	deelneem	[deelneəm]
to pay (vi, vt)	betaal	[betãl]
to permit (vt)	toelaat	[tulãt]
to play (children)	speel	[speəl]
to pray (vi, vt)	bid	[bit]
to promise (vt)	beloof	[beloəf]
to propose (vt)	voorstel	[foərstəl]
to prove (vt)	bewys	[bevajs]
to read (vi, vt)	lees	[leəs]
to receive (vt)	ontvang	[ontfaŋ]
to rent (sth from sb)	huur	[hɪr]
to repeat (say again)	herhaal	[herhãl]
to reserve, to book	bespreek	[bespreək]
to run (vi)	hardloop	[hardloəp]
to save (rescue)	red	[ret]
to say (~ thank you)	sê	[sɛ:]
to see (vt)	sien	[sin]
to sell (vt)	verkoop	[ferkoəp]
to send (vt)	stuur	[stɪr]
to shoot (vi)	skiet	[skit]
to shout (vi)	skreeu	[skriʊ]
to show (vt)	wys	[vajs]
to sign (document)	teken	[tekən]
to sing (vi)	fluit	[flœit]
to sit down (vi)	gaan sit	[χãn sit]
to smile (vi)	glimlag	[χlimlaχ]
to speak (vi, vt)	praat	[prãt]
to steal (money, etc.)	steel	[steəl]
to stop (please ~ calling me)	ophou	[ophæʊ]
to study (vt)	studeer	[studeər]
to swim (vi)	swem	[swem]
to take (vt)	vat	[fat]
to talk to ...	praat met ...	[prãt met ...]
to tell (story, joke)	vertel	[fertəl]
to thank (vt)	dank	[dank]
to think (vi, vt)	dink	[dink]
to translate (vt)	vertaal	[fertãl]
to trust (vt)	vertrou	[fertræʊ]
to try (attempt)	probeer	[probeər]

to turn (e.g., ~ left)	**draai**	[drāi]
to turn off	**afskakel**	[afskakəl]
to turn on	**aanskakel**	[āŋskakəl]
to understand (vt)	**verstaan**	[ferstān]
to wait (vt)	**wag**	[vaχ]
to want (wish, desire)	**wil**	[vil]
to work (vi)	**werk**	[verk]
to write (vt)	**skryf**	[skrajf]

www.ingramcontent.com/pod-product-compliance
Lightning Source LLC
Chambersburg PA
CBHW060024050426
42448CB00012B/2867